Tell Me How You Eat

Food, Power and the Will to Live

AMBER HUSAIN

HUTCHINSON
HEINEMANN

HUTCHINSON HEINEMANN

UK | USA | Canada | Ireland | Australia
India | New Zealand | South Africa

Hutchinson Heinemann is part of the Penguin Random House group of companies
whose addresses can be found at global.penguinrandomhouse.com

Penguin Random House UK,
One Embassy Gardens, 8 Viaduct Gardens, London SW11 7BW

penguin.co.uk

Penguin
Random House
UK

First published 2026

001

Copyright © Amber Husain, 2026

Set in Dante MT Pro 12.1/15.2pt
Typeset by Six Red Marbles UK, Thetford, Norfolk

Printed and bound in Great Britain by Clays Ltd, Elcograf S.p.A.

The authorised representative in the EEA is Penguin Random House Ireland,
Morrison Chambers, 32 Nassau Street, Dublin D02 YH68

A CIP catalogue record for this book is available from the British Library

ISBN: 978-1-529-15433-7

Tell Me How You Eat

For my mother

Contents

Prologue

There are things that are very hard to understand. Frogs fall out of the sky and people fall out of love and somehow, despite all those years of having done it, you have basically forgotten how to eat.

Between the start of 2020 and the end of 2021, I had transitioned from unthinkingly swallowing hundreds of times a day to staring instead, dumbly, into the glare of my own fridge. Pondering the contents inconclusively as though this were the point of my day, I'd close the door, re-open it and start the pondering again.

My boyfriend, Matt, an excellent cook, maintained a certain standard of living. I took odd bites, enjoyed them, but no longer enjoyed the enjoyment. I lost a load of weight and looked pretty weird, but what could I do about that? I could have eaten more, but eating, as I have already said, felt strangely impossible to do.

'Tell me what you eat,' wrote the nineteenth-century politician Jean Anthelme Brillat-Savarin, continuing: 'I will tell you what you are.' He also wrote that dessert without cheese was like a pretty woman with only one eye.

Brillat-Savarin was essentially a lawyer who liked to talk about food, but aspired to be able to 'hold [his] own in conversations with men of science'. He was a child of the Enlightenment, the era of rational thought, when we invented the 'good diet'. The wisdom of the age was that societies could thrive on individuals' pursuit of bodily vigour. To that end, Brillat-Savarin set about writing the *Physiology of Taste* (1825), a now-classic armchair analysis of various food-stuffs. Breaking these down into their (supposed) constituent parts, he attempted to chart their effects on the 'faculty of thought'. He spun from this an image of good, healthy French men, made of turkey, truffles and soup.

Historically, it has mostly proven possible to see through this kind of 'science', which claims an objective, universal goodness for little more than bourgeois entertainment. In the early twentieth century, the sociologist Max Weber skewered the 'clean and solid' ideal of middle-class culinary culture as nothing but public relations – a signal from the bourgeoisie of their relative restraint after the 'glitter and ostentation of feudal magnificence'. Health, as the cultural critic Roland Barthes later observed, is often merely 'the alibi food gives itself' for meaning other things – most often things about status. Writing in 1961, Barthes ridiculed a recent study that marked out the lower classes by their preference for choco-lates, strong perfumes, smooth materials. All to be contrasted with a more refined palate for the bitter, irregular and subtle.

And yet, for the whole of my lifetime, the spirit of Brillat-Savarin has felt quite decisively alive. When I was growing up in the 2000s, *You Are What You Eat* was a popular TV show in which a presenter dressed as a doctor scrutinised 'overweight' people's shit. The logic of this slogan made people all around you look genuinely concerned that schoolkids were made of Turkey Twizzlers, a variety of processed meat made iconic by a TV chef's crusade against it. Teenage girlhood was a Venti Caramel Macchiato and your parents were the cabbage soup diet. Things have changed, by which I mean the relevant foods, but the logic remains the same. Between the start of 2020 and the end of 2021, Lao Gan Ma chili crisp made for a man in the know, tins of fish for hot girls, and the oily fruits of laurel trees (still!) for fiscally careless millennials.

With respect to my own new diet of paralysed fridge contemplation, you might have said I was what I *didn't* eat. What, in that case, did 'nothing' make me? Presumably nothing good.

When the term *anorexia* first arose in Britain, France and the USA, it meant you were an obstinate young woman. In the early nineteenth century, psychiatrists described a morbid medical state of self-starvation which they parsed as a form of adolescent rebellion. Otherwise well-behaved girls seemed to be spending their days at home only to reject its obvious comforts. What reason could they have beyond a wildly annoying need for parental attention?

With the rise of modern feminism, public thinkers have tried to redeem this tale of misbehaviour, restyling churlish theatrics as legitimate *dissent*. Psychologists in the 1970s, taking up the notion of a daughter's disease, saw women's self-starvation less as a childish 'acting out' than an understandable response to family dynamics. Anorexia, they thought, was a symptom of the threat to young women's power to define themselves. The German writer Hilde Bruch and Argentinian Salvador Minuchin wrote of daughters overwhelmed by overbearing mothers. These girls sought thinness perhaps for a sense of personal achievement, perhaps just as something to call their own.

Feminists of the 1980s offered alternative perspectives on a similarly framed situation: women, they agreed, had been cheated of their autonomy, but what if the culprit wasn't parents but patriarchy? And what if starving, in the incipient age of the waif, wasn't protest but surrender? For the writer Kim Chernin, anorexia was the logical endpoint of patriarchal economic pressures – a compulsive attempt to avoid the financially ruinous fate of the wife abandoned for her fatness. For psychoanalyst Susie Orbach, anorexics hall-of-mirrored an impossible social standard: the ideal of the subservient female without any needs. A wafer-thin woman, for Orbach, was an extreme but not an exception: she was nothing but an icon of women's diminishment in general.

Whether we have read the failure to eat as a rebuke to patriarchal ideals, or a clumsy overinvestment in them, it is almost always *the female condition* that underwrites the narrative. Women, we understand, are engaged in an uphill struggle to determine what they are. No wonder, we conclude, they would express themselves through food. You are, after all, what you eat.

There are things that are very hard to understand, so we adopt other people's understandings. We wear them around like beautiful, if ill-fitting, shoes we hope will give us some footing in normal society. When a woman stops eating, rote explanations are repurposed and tweaked, documentaries and memoirs ensue. We want these to perfect a redemption arc of suffocated childhood, feminist self-discovery and buttery self-acceptance. To love your own womanly flesh, we are advised, is to transcend the society that hates you.

We sense we should be grateful for this happy side-effect of having been made so unwell.

I would have liked to be able to contribute my own evidence to this canon, but I wouldn't have been telling the truth. I have no doubt that there are women who have starved to death in resentment of their mothers, or in fear of chubby destitution. Affronts to women's autonomy are real, ongoing and liable to make a person ill. I could not say, however, that my own trouble with eating felt connected with any of that. In 2020, I was twenty-eight years old and, if far from well off, at least financially independent. My mother wasn't controlling and, even if she had been, I'd long since flown her nest. To the extent that I was interested in beauty, I was very well aware that my thinness wasn't it. I felt, in other words, no drive to assert or define myself through food, through my body, or indeed its disappearance. No desire to be perfectly female or monstrously, rebelliously thin. What I ate seemed entirely at odds with both what I was and what I wanted to be. There must, I assumed, have been other possible explanations.

And what if there were? Would these represent only more filler for the catalogue of personal struggles? Or in fact, nothing less than a conceptual affront to our very under-standing of food? For if it is possible that someone might starve not in service but in spite of their sense of self, we are forced to humour a schism between the 'eats' and the 'is'. Such a person will tell you what they eat (or what they don't), and when it comes to what they are, you must admit you are none the wiser. What would it mean, in that case, to have to contemplate food as something other than a font, or a mark, of personal value?

There are some who hold that the failure to eat shouldn't be given much thought at all – at least not in a way that aspires to draw any insight. 'We'd like to believe', wrote Alice Gregory in the *New Yorker* in 2013, 'that such unhinged myopia would have psychological roots in trauma or in some sinister personal history but usually it doesn't.' The most honest kind of writing, for Gregory, would instead show anorexia for how 'profoundly boring' it really is – a disease of 'slowly suicidal obsessives who avoid other people and expend 95 per cent of their mental energy counting the calories in green vegetables'.

Gregory's feelings were, and are, at least up to date with the ideas of the current medical mainstream. With the third edition of the American Psychiatric Association's *Diagnostic and Statistical Manual of Mental Disorders*, published in 1980, eating disorders were enshrined in biomedical rubric less as a thing to understand and laboriously work through than as something to recognise and swiftly correct. Rather than theorising tangled histories of anorexic feeling, the DSM-3 simply listed and described a standard set of symptoms and behaviours. In the DSM-5, the latest version of the handbook, these are roughly summarisable as follows: restriction of food (A), leading to very low weight (B), and resistance to reversing this trajectory (C).

There is obvious appeal for certain patients, not to mention their long-maligned mothers, in efforts to clinically neutralise the scandal of excessive non-eating. Rather than serving sufferers back the vomit of their pasts, the facts of their dysfunctional families or the ceaseless degradation of their gender, clinicians today speak to patients of things like genetic predisposition, hormonal dysregulation and personality profile. They acknowledge certain basic empirical facts – like how boys get anorexia too. They promise verifiable solutions in the form of drugs and behavioural re-training.

One obvious drawback to treatments like these is that they don't really work. Recovery rates from anorexia in standard clinical settings are acknowledged to be low, relapse and fatality high. While it can be soothing to ignore the difficult context in which an illness develops, blaming instead certain predisposing factors and treating only the symptoms, lifelong symptom management and meaningful transformation are not the same thing. While the latter implies a completely new relationship with the world, which requires that we question its dysfunctions, the former merely gives us tools for accepting those dysfunctions, living blandly on. If we grant that genetics might have a role to play in why someone develops a terror of eating, we are nonetheless left with questions of *why now, why here*? That the Covid-19 pandemic saw a surge in eating disorder cases cannot be rationalised in terms of genetics.

Still, the medical professionals who were asked about this surge jumped to emphasise their patients' hard-wired weaknesses. In the *Guardian*, Dr Agnes Ayton, chair of the Eating Disorder Faculty at the UK's Royal College of Psychiatrists, pointed to the anorexic population's excessive need for control. The *New York Times* quoted Dr Walter Kaye, founder and executive director of the eating disorders programme at the University of California San Diego, who explained that 'people who end up with eating disorders tend to be anxious and stress sensitive – they don't deal well with uncertainty'. It makes a certain practical sense for medics to focus on traits – on individual bodies rather than the turmoil that surrounds them. It is also extremely convenient for pharmaceutical companies, who profit from simply drugging these traits away. It is convenient, most of all, for the political establishment, who need not account for a disease that proliferates in step with its decisions.

Though I struggled to relate to the theories of bratty girls with tyrant mothers, or women with a slavish attraction to thinness, I wasn't content to stop asking the kinds of questions that had led to these theories' emergence: questions of agency, autonomy and power. In order to land on these kinds of hypotheses, feminists and psychoanalytic thinkers had had to attend to the difficult subject of the world in which we live. What kind of life must you be living, they asked, to find in starvation a preferable way of being? What kind of cages define your era, your race, your social class? Are you in one? Did you build it yourself? Unlike medical descriptions of disease, which extrapolate a patient's 'personality type' from how they behave while ill, analytic thought recognises that people are changed, constantly and strangely, by the things that happen around them. I may have become, for example, a 'slowly suicidal obsessive', channelling previously lively brainpower into staring into my fridge, but in a former life I had cared about all kinds of other things.

Not long previously I had cared about a socialist Labour Party's election campaign, spent the winter of 2019 knocking on doors, hosting ring-arounds and making the case for an anti-austerity programme. In early 2020 I had given myself and my salary to a strike, flinging rain-soaked leaflets around in the interests of higher education. It alarmed but also fascinated me that mere months later all I could think about was food – how to approach it, how to avoid it without too much fuss. Only by suspending the pleasure of eating could I seem to find relief, feel myself exempt from something awful. Only what? I wanted to name this awfulness, to understand the spur to such a vacuous non-existence.

This is not the kind of thing you are invited to try and do in most contemporary eating disorder therapies. I learnt this the tedious way when my body mass index earnt me a place on an NHS treatment programme. After politely declining the offer of hospital 'daycare' – a total surrender of adult life to supervised eating routines – I started a more palatable-sounding four-month weekly group therapy course. I liked the idea of group therapy. I hoped that the insights of others – their stories, their desires – might finally shed some light on my own. That perhaps, in non-judgemental solidarity, we'd give our difficulties context; move, however slowly, towards a kind of therapeutic understanding.

Perhaps I should have known that 'MANTRA', the Maudsley Model of Anorexia Nervosa Treatment for Adults, would have the kind of interest in our insights and desires that Rentokil has in bedbugs. The treatment, after all, was named for a hospital named for a man who preached that mental illness was a form of 'moral insanity'. For the Victorian psychiatrist Henry Maudsley, the members of this group would have been classed as biologically degenerate, fit for social life only on the condition that we learn to discipline our madness. The aim was not to examine our inner lives, but instead to subject the behaviours they wrought to efficient extermination.

MANTRA, much like the other primary NHS treatment options – cognitive behavioural therapy and specialist supportive clinical management – is a 'cognitive-interpersonal treatment'. It prides itself as biologically informed and empirically based, drawing on neuroimaging, neuropsychological, social cognitive and personality trait research. Its premise is that anorexia arises from certain inbuilt tendencies – sensitive, anxious, obsessional – and that it is maintained by rigid, perfectionist 'information processing styles', emotional and social impairments, false beliefs about the illness, the enabling behaviours of others and the biological effects of starvation on the brain. The idea is to try and teach all this to anorexic patients in weekly group 'collaborative' sessions. The hope is that they will recognise the error in themselves and learn to see the world like normal people.

There was very little opportunity, here, to speak in continuous prose. The therapists leading the group were assured that all they needed to know about us had already been established in a lab. They carried at all times a big blue book which described in large type who the scientists thought we were, and the specific sequences of exercises needed to right our misbehaviour. The literature describing the model and its evidence base insists that when it comes to anorexics, 'history taking takes time and reveals little of note'. Nothing we said ourselves was to be taken seriously, only categorised as features of our pathology.

On Day One, we sat in a circle at the centre of which were two jars surrounded by marbles. One was labelled 'anorexia thoughts', the other 'rational thoughts'. We were invited to cultivate a practice, throughout our time in the programme, of constant thought-surveillance; the idea was to have us measure our madness in marbles just as the therapists measured us in kilos. I think the simple pleasure of dropping balls in jar number two was meant to motivate us to think like 'rational' people. I imagine this was supposed to make us gain weight, which would verify that everything was fine.

Each session involved a handful of tasks, designed to have us prove our deficiencies to ourselves. We might, for example, be instructed to summarise points from a basic newspaper article. This was supposed to show us how bad we were at 'seeing the bigger picture'. Or we might be asked to quickly draw lines through the centre of various shapes, proving our inability to tolerate imprecision. Often, as certain group members pointed out, we would actually do well at these tasks, even if we struggled to apply the same agility to how we ate. Those who voiced such objections, however, stood accused of not being 'open' to the programme's evidence-based wisdom. This resistance, we were told, was evidence in itself of our rigid, irrational minds. We learnt to stay quiet, put marbles in jars, apologise for ourselves.

The environment was essentially one of Total Administration. Not only was our speech restricted to the context of infantilising tasks, but so was the point of these tasks restricted to the pursuit of certain predetermined outcomes. Once we had understood how badly we were made, and how much worse we had made ourselves by starving, it was assumed we'd be sufficiently scared, or sufficiently ashamed, to *simply not*. Once we had been given an education in the meaning of healthy eating, it was assumed we'd want to be healthy. It was assumed that the kinds of principles that underpin evidence-based medicine – measurable goals, 'best-practice', verifiable progress – would also be the kinds of things that motivated us. Of course, we none of us starved because we thought it was right. We did it because the alternative felt unbearable.

Even, that is, we chosen few who had made it onto the course, in part, for our *readiness to change*. When I had first been assessed for treatment, I asked the interviewing therapist what it was that made me 'qualified', as she put it, beyond my clinically alarming bodyweight. The hospital did not offer this treatment, I was told, to patients who weren't considered 'ready'; who on interview seemed less likely to cooperate, less likely to 'succeed', less likely to be value for money. In voicing out loud this quiet part, the therapist revealed a certain in-built expectation of resistance. The resistance, perhaps, that has the Maudsley model's architects compare their own efforts to educate patients with 'flogging a dead horse'. After a couple of months, I got tired of being flogged and left them to flog away without me.

My next idea, now in the third year of illness, was to turn to a world of bigger budgets and fewer predetermined outcomes; a place where healthcare funding poured into the unknown. I applied to take part in a clinical trial at an NHS research facility. The study aimed to explore the potential of psychedelic-assisted therapy for treating anorexic patients. At two-week intervals over a six-week period, participants would be given three different doses of psilocybin – the active compound produced by magic mushrooms – and psychotherapeutic support with talking through their experiences on the drugs. Where MANTRA comes at patients with instructions – how to eat, how to think, how to see – this study was both more modest and more ambitious in its aims. It did not presume to offer a normative vision of the world, but proposed instead that the experience of tripping might offer the patient their own, new vision – new ways of understanding the root of their malaise, new ideas for how they might approach it. Like psychoanalysis – an art as much as a science of the mind – psychedelic medicine remains at least open to a more expansive, less 'objective' therapeutic use. This is in part because it takes as a given that the things that make us suffer live largely in the realm of the unconscious – a hinterland unmeasurable by scientific tools.

At its ancient roots, and as practised across the Americas and Global South, psychedelic healing has offered channels of communication with the natural and spirit worlds. The power of the drug is here connected with its ritual use – with the constellation of relationships this produces, beyond the self. It derives from thought worlds where illness has been understood as issuing from imbalance between communities and nature, with psychedelics imagined as a route to restoring a kind of ecological balance.

The adoption of psychedelics in the modern and contemporary West has involved some rebranding. It should perhaps come as no surprise that in a hypercapitalist context, the magic of mind-revelation would be valued for its potential less in spiritual-ecological relations than in projects of self-improvement. There was certainly some effort, within the American counterculture of the 1960s, to put the drugs to more collectivist uses, awakening the robotic, consumerist mind to our connection with others and the cosmos. Yet it was also a commonplace of psychedelic 'research' at the time to want to expand the minds of a business elite. Shrooms were introduced to the West by the vice president of J. P. Morgan, with a view to enhancing the problem-solving mind and disrupting its destructive patterns of thought; they have since become a favoured plaything of Silicon Valley's smallest-minded hegemons.

Similarly, Western psychedelic therapy has typically focused on healing one body at a time – whether from diagnosed conditions like anxiety, addiction or depression, or from the kind of spiritual void a person perceives as holding them back in life.

There is plenty of reason to be sceptical of this bastardisation process, which threatens to reinforce the idea of illness and its opposite as more-or-less private matters. A neurobiology-forward research culture, geared to the profit imperatives of tech and pharmaceutical companies, has reduced a set of mystical substances known for their social power to a set of chemical compounds whose framing as an individual 'cure' shores up their value as intellectual property. Yet even the most medicalised of psychedelic therapies has trouble reducing itself to mere individual biochemistry.

Psychedelic medicine stays alert to the fact that knowing your own problems is hard – not because you are cognitively defective, but because the unconscious is obscure by definition. It is an insight drawn from the world of psychoanalysis, in which it is understood that our thoughts are never purely rational or irrational in nature – that inner life is always a mixture of the two; that it is made not just of cognitive capacities but fantasies, fears and desires. The work of psychoanalysis is gradually to bring these forces into a space where the patient can meet them. If we open ourselves to the potential of *psyche-delics*, etymologically 'mind-manifesting' substances, we are liable to slip into a hallucinatory zone where the sources of our pain can be perceived. And if we are hopelessly attached to trivialities that do not serve us well, the shrooms, if we are lucky, might instil a sense of awe that puts such things in perspective.

Photographs on the website for the study I applied for suggested a faintly comical effort to reproduce the kind of controlled LSD 'research' pioneered in the 1950s. One-time American spy Al Hubbard, for example, catering to a number of politicians and proto tech-entrepreneurs, would feed his participants acid in a special room, play them music, show them paintings and wait for them to meet their problem-solving God. On my laptop screen, what was unmistakably a hospital bed in the middle of a hospital floor was draped with colourful throws and surrounded by panels that mimicked a sparkling forest scene. Where plastic filing cabinets would ordinarily go were little wooden chests of drawers. On top of these were a speaker and two Himalayan salt lamps, theatrically oversized, pink.

After several weeks of physical and psychological screening, I prepared to take my first dose. I cannot say I was numb, at this time, to the situation's absurdity. As I sat in a darkened hospital room, just like the one in the picture, on a mountain of embroidered cushions, I was given not a knobbly mushroom to grip between my teeth, but three clean and odourless pills. These had not been extracted from fungus, but synthesised in a lab, officially in the interests of 'precision', but also – a thought that was hard to suppress – in the interests of a biotechnology company.

I was occasionally unnerved, disenchanted, by the study's obsession with measuring stuff in my skull. The days before and after I was given my drugs, I would be studded with electrical sensors or bundled into MRI machines for hours of brain surveillance. Often, I worried that in signing up for this trial I had simply returned to the same old nightmare – crude biomedical banality, only this time with incense and drum recordings. I knew that all research of this nature was pressured to justify itself to its funders, who privilege a precise and objective language of biomarkers and brains; the kinds of things that many scientists believe can be analysed out of context. Perhaps this is why reports on the use of psychedelics for anorexics refer to changes in the brain's 'top-down predictive networks', its regions of 'self-referential processing'. Archetypically individualist in focus, they point to how psilocybin can disrupt the user's preconceived beliefs about their own body, or how they make these beliefs more flexible by shattering their very sense of self.

This was not, however, the tenor of my experience on the drugs, which felt about as far from a body-image course or neurological fix as the divine feels far from a jar of 'rational thought' marbles. Nor was this the tone of conversations with my two 'study guides'. These were mental health professionals of a kind who saw no need, when discussing the workings of the mind, to translate it onto regions of my brain. Both sat alongside me for the duration of each of my eight-hour trips. They told me from the start that the mushrooms wouldn't make me feel better, but that they might start to help me understand what it would take for me to do so. After each dose, they would spend several hours with me the following day to help me try and conjure some thoughts: what I had seen, what I had felt, what I wanted to do with it all.

This can be hard after you've surfaced from a nine-to-five day of all but losing your mind. The first 'significant' dose I received sent me straight into a twinkling hell. There seemed to be no thought, just sensation – mostly an objectless dread. I felt some initial concern that, Mushroom forbid, the sensation would last all day, but the concept of a 'day' soon escaped me. As I felt myself squeezed and rolled through recurring panes of glass, time felt threateningly non-linear, a spiral's infinite grin. I was vaguely aware there'd been a 'morning', when I'd brought myself to this place, but the world in which I had done so no longer felt viable or real. I asked my guides a couple of times if they could make it stop. 'Not really,' they replied, which seemed about right since they probably weren't real either.

This was a problem, as I remained distinctly aware that at something called 6pm Matt would be coming to pick me up. How was he supposed to collect this mind without a body? Or perhaps there was a body, but he'd find it switched off and freak out because that wasn't the plan. My guides instructed me to trust them, trust the mushrooms, trust the 'process', but the 'process' seemed irrelevant now. The very idea of an 'eating disorder' belonged to a dimension of which I, a mere stream of sensation with no mouth, was no longer a working part. The feeling was something like paralysis without muscle – a feeling I tried to express but all the language on earth seemed to have drained into outer space on a tide of sounds like 'porridge' or 'gobble' or 'Robert'. Resisting this loss of words, I began to try to write something like this paragraph in my head, imagining how I would tell it to my friends if I ever returned. I tried to impose a past tense on things to secure my spot in a world where all this would be in the past. As though I could write my way back to life despite my conviction that I was, in fact, dead. For a while I tried to ask, 'Does it have to be bad?', and then I gave up. There was no one left to reach and nothing to say and nowhere to go but inward.

What struck my guides about this was not the feeling's otherworldly, or otherwise exceptional, badness. 'Futility', as they put it in our next-day debrief, was nothing special to them. *No one left to reach and nothing to say and nowhere to go but inward.* Like Freudians, my psychedelic guides were attuned to the collective nature of suffering, interested in finding the 'common unhappiness' beneath the hysterical misery. They wanted their participants to answer the kinds of questions I wanted to ask. Where could I locate the futility, they asked, other than outer space? Where might I have felt this way in normal, terrestrial life?

While it is plausible that I could have felt impotent just by virtue of my own personality, or by virtue of my female identity, these were not the associations I made when I recalled that sensation of psychedelic hell. If that hopelessness felt reminiscent of anything, it was the aftertaste of recent, somewhat political, events.

Not, I should say, like the 2019 election loss itself, which had tasted, not completely unpleasantly, of corner-shop cava and snot. There had been something sweetly convivial in the choric wails of despair on the night all that went down. At least for that evening, the organised Left still knew what we were doing: we were wailing in despair. I am talking about the days after, when our sinuses had cleared, along with any sense of the meaning of words and ideas.

Until then, for at least a few years, certain ambitions had seemed straightforward: green industry, workers' rights, free education, free healthcare, free movement, money for making art. Now, we were supposed to accept that this was, always had been, *unelectable extremism*. The media did it, partly. And whereas before we had thought we could get around that by knocking on every door in the country, suddenly the sensible thing to have done looked a lot like nothing at all. This thought didn't taste like cheap cava; it tasted like shit, and that is a taste that lingers.

Which perhaps is why hopelessness also felt like the sensible response to the events of the year that followed. When people struggled to eat in the time of Covid, Dr Walter Kaye speculated that such people were reacting badly to a moment of 'uncertainty'. But wasn't the pandemic, in many respects, also a time of heightened certainty? Of clarity, for example, about the outsized power of governments to reinforce the existing hierarchy of lives? Of certainty about the extent of miserable working and housing conditions; the powerlessness of those who had to endure them? Was it not possible that the declared 'inevitability' of these things could put a person off their food? Just as easily, for instance, as wanting to be either gorgeously or freakishly thin?

Until I started asking these questions, the only efforts to historicise eating disorders I had read connected their rise in the twentieth-century West with an intensification of beauty standards. I had not considered that their fast pro-liferation had also trailed the rise of a social and economic world governed by vast, impersonal 'systems'; systems that we, mere people, can neither predict nor control. We are told that within this arrangement, the best we can do is play the game and try to benefit ourselves; that trying to band together to make things less unfair would be tra-gically counterproductive. We have no time, it seems, to notice the ways this makes us ill. We come to believe that political inertia is an ordinary state. For the writer Cynthia Cruz, anorexia might then be read like any other disease of despair. 'How do we resist a system we cannot see,' she asks, 'a system we are told does not exist?'

Anorexics might either descend into our own symptomatic relief – our disinvestment from the world and its food – or try to fight the illness simply by forcing ourselves to consume. You are what you eat, and *what you are*, we have been led to believe, is all there is. We dutifully gain some weight, are then confused when we lose it again. We do not do ourselves the courtesy of asking if the problem might be more than our relationship with ourselves.

If, then, I thought, the things that drive ordinary people to freeze in the face of food do extend beyond the question of 'what we are', perhaps they might also include the difficult question of *what we can do* – the question of our capacity, or lack thereof, to act upon the world. This would take us beyond the realm of autonomy, and into the realm of power. Improving our societal relationship with food, in that case, would take more than self-affirmations, cognitive and behavioural tricks for perfecting some idealised diet. Presumably it would matter not just *what you ate* but the context in which you did it – whether the act of eating gave you hope or gave you hell.

There is a certain reticence, in feminist circles, of treating any difficulty with food as though it reached beyond the self; as though it might spring from any motive other than attention-seeking, self-destruction or vanity. It is understandable, sometimes. Particularly in the extreme case of anorexia, people fear they will 'glamorise' something they believe should be held in contempt, what they see as women's traitorous self-deprivation. Anorexia, writes Alice Gregory, disguises as a virtue what is in fact 'insane . . . inhumane'. The writer Lisa Appignanesi, in a book that is otherwise critical of women's pathologisation, incriminates those who 'prefer to categorise their condition as a saintly protest against the consumer culture rather than a mental disorder'. The journalist Emmeline Clein, in general a proponent of listening to those who struggle with eating, refuses to 'buy' the writer Chris Kraus's suggestion that anorexia might represent an 'escape from the role of citizen, a role [Kraus] sees as inevitably complicit in injustice'. In Kraus's *Aliens & Anorexia*, the author/narrator despairs of food that has never been 'touched with understanding'; of 'bodies of imprisoned animals', sold in air-conditioned cases. *Why do I hate everything?* she asks herself, as the edible products of exploited labour begin to smell like 'bills and coins and plastic'. Kraus floats the idea of the anorexic as drawing an 'intellectual equation between a culture's food and the *entire social order*'. But '[o]nce all the good girls are dead,' Clein protests in her 2024 book *Dead Weight*, 'who does she want writing?' Clein wishes Kraus would just 'take a mallet to a crab, dip meat in butter'. She wishes the political philosopher Simone Weil, who also refused to eat, would 'put mayo on a chunk of bread instead of dying'.

What goes unreflected on here is not just the question of whether some 'good girls' might in fact prefer to die than suffer what the world has dealt them (including its mayonnaise); there is also the more basic fact that describing an illness as an 'escape' from undesirable political conditions is not the same as calling it a political solution. To the contrary, there is nothing more depoliticising than whittling your social cosmos down to the microcosm of your body. But just because there is nothing saintly, transformative or artful in this pose, should we ignore the idea that its originating context might be a political matter? Writers like Clein, who speak profusely of 'politics' in relation to eating disorders, appear to find it safer to reduce the meaning of the word to the politics of feminine beauty standards. For Clein, to speak of eating disorders as a reaction to society's beauty ideal shows us a straightforward route to liberation, but to speak of them as a reaction to 'society itself' represents a kind of nihilism. I suppose that, unlike the entire social order, at least the desire to be hot sounds like something we might be able to talk ourselves out of. 'I want to sit cross-legged', writes Clein, addressing an imagined sister in disorder, 'and talk about the thoughts that almost killed us, until we decided not to let them.'

The idea that simply changing one's thoughts might suffice as a political solution would seem to be testament precisely to our era's political torpor – a widespread failure to imagine 'resistance' as meaning anything more than privately transcending the dominant social narratives. So hard is it to imagine the possibility of *transforming* the social order, that when a thinker like Kraus (who speaks not even of transformation, only critique) so much as mentions said order, she stands accused of having given up on politics altogether.

That said, Clein is right that it is difficult to think of transformation when you're hungry or dead. It is one thing to say that you will eat when you've worked out how to change the world, another to survive for long enough to see the process through. Even Freud, whose life's work emblematised the notion that illness harbours meaning, warned against his own talking cure as a first resort for anorexic patients. 'The starving girl,' he wrote, 'whatever the origin of her symptoms, needs more radical help than psychotherapy can at first provide.'

So it seemed I was going to have to find some inspiration to live that was also an inspiration to eat; or perhaps an inspiration to eat that was also an inspiration to live. Surely, I began to reason, there were ways of experiencing food beyond what Kraus, albeit perceptively, described: food as a weapon of society; eating as surrender to its norms; eating as complicity in a system of injustice. If there were, I would have to look in places far from the world of MANTRA, which taught that proper nutrition was simply a form of civic duty. Places far from the mediatised dogma that you *are*, that you amount to, the value of your dietary choices. If we ate the right foods, the MANTRA therapists advised, in carefully measured amounts, we'd transform into the right kind of beings – deflationary proof of institutions' conditional approach to granting humanity.

Modern medical treatments for anorexia proceed from the idea that you feed a person first and (possibly) attend to their humanity later. If they succeed in filling patients' stomachs, it is often with the help of sedative medication, systems of punishment and restraint, and force-feeding by nasogastric tube. None of these measures seems particularly likely to nourish a hopeful worldview, if that is indeed what is at stake. They make us fit for a world perhaps we do not want to live in; perhaps they make us hate it even more. They ask us to lower our bar for what we take to be a 'life' – not much more than a healthy BMI. Starving, I saw, might offer a reprieve from this vision of life, but if you wanted a way to live otherwise, you would have to find new ways to eat.

'Eat and you will start to think differently,' the MANTRA therapists said. 'Eat and you'll start to feel better.' Perhaps they had had a point after all, just not for the reasons they imagined.

In the weeks and months that followed the discussions with my psychedelic guides, I tried to look for new ways of eating. I turned well away from manuals and sunk myself instead in the stories of other people. People whose commitment to food seemed connected, in some way, with what they hoped to achieve; how they imagined political futures better than those into which they'd been born. People for whom eating was, or had been, more than an act of self-definition. I considered the lives of those who had inspired me before I had ceased to be inspired by much. People whose life's work had been to protect other people's jobs or to make it so that women wouldn't get burnt at the stake. Or so that kids could have breakfast or lesbians the chance to fuck each other in peace.

It is only through the lives and eating habits of such people that I began to make more sense not only of the ways I had been struggling to eat, but also the ways I'd kept on eating. From feminist hunger strikers and eco socialist cooks, I learnt how methods of restriction, including my own, could exceed mere refusal, connecting with positive visions for a more just nourishment. Through radical poets, I found that there were different ways of gorging – not just in bourgeois self-love but with an unchained, polymorphous eroticism. I discovered there were many different ways to feed another person – to choke, to coerce and to care; how 'love' could be a name for all of the above, such that *made with love* was often insufficient. In the eating habits of others more inspired than myself I recognised ways in which, for all my relative despair, I had in fact been keeping myself alive. Ways I had refused to completely let go of that romance you can have with the world. I began to understand, more generally, how political imaginations can be shaped, as well as disfigured, by the ways in which we eat; the ways we are sometimes made to. There is much to be gained, it transpires, from thinking of food as more than what makes us responsible, sophisticated, 'well'.

I would like to have been able to write one of those books you might have read about the magic of healing through food. Unfortunately, it seems there is nothing inherently healing about it. Not when what passes for eating might include, for example, getting stuffed with liquid calories through a tube. Nor are there particular meals I'd recommend for your virtue or health; to comfort your soul or mystically *restore your faith in the world*. As Barthes put it, there is 'no natural item of food that signifies anything itself'; no prescribable route to moral rectitude or strength. When you imagine that salvation consists in mere bodily health – the kind you can swallow – you swallow nothing more than a lie.

And yet, if salvation consists instead in building a better world, what if eating could, at least, prime our vision for that place? If anorexia – a personal refusal of food – and the 'good diet' – its overinflation with personal value – together represent two aspects of the same, ubiquitous curling inward, what would it mean to engage the question of *how we eat* in the imaginative work of turning outwards? In looking towards a more liveable, collectively organised world?

We would have to consider less the content than the 'spirit' of eating; the spirit in which a movement feeds itself. We would have to pay attention to what happens in that interval when our mouths are full or filled; when there is little opportunity to lie . . .

I

You Don't

A sandwich can involve many things at once: lettuce, regret, tomatoes, fried tofu, maybe some pickles, slicks of butter, despair, ennui.

Maybe you like sandwiches, though. The one I just described at least looked uncontroversial. Apart from (some would argue) the tofu, which no one could see from the outside anyway, there could be few overt signals in a big white bap that I was some kind of bourgeois arsehole – like the kind who lunches on 'street food' made by white entrepreneurs in pedestrianised enclaves overrun by wooden forks. At least it signalled I was not the kind of person who doesn't care about life and brings an underwhelming squirl of cold spaghetti out for lunch from a stained Tupperware box.

Maybe you, too, like the idea that a sandwich seems honest, which was hard for me to project because I was supposed to be anorexic, and that, as we know, is a textbook liar's disease. I liked that the sandwich made my veins feel fuller after I'd fasted, under instruction, until four in the afternoon. I liked the way the not-so-sweet tomato juice turned the bread into a moist, acid sponge. But then there are the things it is harder to like: the regret, the despair, the ennui.

It seems likely there are aspects of this complex relationship with sandwiches you find more relatable than others. Perhaps you'd go for bacon and sourdough or a brand-name plastic bread. Perhaps you have never been clinically diagnosed with an eating disorder, and class yourself as only moderately disturbed by the meanings attached to your diet. It is extremely unlikely, though possible, that you typically take your sandwiches after fasting, under instruction, until four in the afternoon. The only reason I did that was because I was participating in a clinical trial, assessing the value of psilocybin-assisted therapy for anorexia patients.

The research team had needed me to spend an extremely hungry hour in an MRI scanner. The instruction, then, was not to eat a thing until it was done. I'd be amazed, the study coordinator insisted, by the difference hunger can make to regional brain activity. I took this to imply that any sins would probably find me out. Stolen mouthfuls would flourish under the scanner like love-bites on my prefrontal cortex.

This paranoia may have had something to do with the fact that until the study had started, most of my interactions with the team had revolved around proving my condition. I'd needed doctors' notes to confirm my DSM-5 diagnosis, and to confirm that their own attempts at treatment had failed to undo it. A series of interviews and physical exams had been arranged to check that I was all the things you had to be: restricting my food (A), of a very low weight (B), and resistant to reversing this trajectory (C).

Yet here I was, not entirely resistant to reversing this trajectory, or I'd never have signed up for the study. My presence was proof, in fact, of some commitment to a reversal – at least enough for me to have taken some powerful drugs.

Drugs so powerful, in fact, that on two of the three occasions I'd been given them, I'd started to believe I was dead. I'd been prepared to come back, after hours of what the researchers called 'primitive agony', and see what more the mushrooms had to reveal. I'd returned, at the end of all this, to spend one last hour in a brain-scanning tube, hungrily watching videos of food and rating how much I enjoyed them. I was prepared to play along with the seemingly fruitless task of assigning numbers to fruit, of quantifying my feelings about how the flow of chocolate sauce compared with the churn of a pencil sharpener.

More to the point, I was committed enough to be eating an actual sandwich. To have *wanted* to eat the sandwich even before the white coats finally gave me the nod at four. The urge to commit sandwich adultery when I was supposed to be anorexic was, I supposed, kind of funny. Had I not been there precisely because desire is a complex thing, I might also have found it quite comforting. I might have wondered, in fact, if I'd cured myself just by signing up for the trial. I might have wondered if, now, when we were wrapping things up and I was wrapping my mouth around a sandwich, this meant the cure was almost complete. This kind of eating, after all, was a category violation of criterion (A) – the one where anorexics must restrict their intake of food. All I would need now was to eat enough to breach criterion (B) – the one about low weight – and I'd be DSM-5-official happy.

But like I said before, I was not sold on the idea that my daily struggle to eat was a struggle with food alone. My suspicion that it wasn't was only reinforced by the food-free experience of hell I had been shown in psychedelic space. I had been given to believe that my problem might, for example, have something to do with an overwhelming sense of the pointless; the exhaustion of any belief that life was in fact worth feeding.

There are people who would never eat a sandwich, I thought, but whose body weight, for whatever reason, never reaches 'very low'. Sometimes these people are so resistant to eating sandwiches that the mere invitation to do so makes it hard for them to breathe. There are also people who really, really do not want to eat sandwiches but for whatever reason eat them anyway. No one calls these people anorexic, and therefore no one offers them therapeutic shrooms, yet still we all have something in common. We all have relationships with sandwiches that give us some level of grief.

People like me, who had been through (A), (B) and (C), and were now engaged in eating, were not supposed to relate to these other people's complex relationship with sandwiches. The DSM-5 is not interested in collapsing its own boxes. The DSM-5 will try to tell you who you are or who you have been, not the nature of your experience. The DSM-5 would like to know if you are a person who wants to eat, or if you are a person who doesn't. It doesn't acknowledge that you can want, and be suspicious of, the same thing at once. It doesn't care if you want the tofu, the lettuce and the bread, but not the despair or ennui. It doesn't care if you want to get better, but only if it's possible for life to get better too. It certainly doesn't care if, after a large dose of mushrooms, you decide you want to be nourished, but still are not quite convinced that being nourished will be worth it.

This, in any case, was the state in which I looked forward to eating my sandwich: one of consent to at least finding out if things could be better than they were. This finding out, I recognised, would require me to eat, and eating, as we know, can be nice. Eating, though, was no guarantee that anything much would change but my weight.

In my experience of more orthodox eating disorder treatment, many professionals insist it is objectively possible to feel better simply by eating. They have a pet experiment to prove it – a study conducted in the 1940s. I thought about this study as I bit into the bread.

A few weeks into my course of group 'therapy' on an NHS treatment programme, the group was treated to a special educational session with a dietician called Harriet. Harriet could hardly wait to tell us about the Minnesota Starvation Experiment – a study she told us repeatedly that she *loved*. Harriet wished they could replicate the study today but 'you'd never get the permission'. This maybe should have raised some red flags about Harriet. Still, we heard her out. Heard her present the evidence for why 'feeding first' was the way to cure an eating disorder.

The Minnesota Starvation Experiment took place towards the end of the Second World War. In 1944, civilians in occupied Europe had been starved, and needed to be re-fed. Those who hadn't been blasted to bits had been living, just about, on mere bread and potatoes, and only God, at this point, knew what their shrunken stomachs could handle. In a bid to establish the optimal diet for bringing a person back to life, the American scientist Ancel Keys set about designing an experimental rehearsal of the refeeding process. For this, he needed healthy subjects to refeed, which meant mercilessly starving them first.

The thirty-six test subjects in the Minnesota Starvation Experiment had been chosen from a pool of male volunteers.

For six months, they were subjected to a 'war conditions' diet, built around cabbage and potatoes with splashes of bean-and-pea soup. Quantities were controlled right down to the drops of vinegar on salad. As the participants were progressively deprived over the weeks and their bodies began to eat themselves, a curious thing began to happen to these otherwise 'normal' men: all of them – Harriet actually beamed at this part – began to act like anorexic girls.

Which is to say, as their bodies underwent the biological assault of malnourishment, their minds grew erratic, impatient and, crucially, weird about food. As their blood emptied of sugar and protein, the Minnesota men squirreled cookbooks under their beds and sliced thimbles of food into flakes. Like would-be ballerinas they mastered ritual eating and perfected bad moods. On excursions from the research facility, they watched other people eat in restaurants with a lunatic kind of joy. The friendliest souls turned solipsistic, bickered, bitched, bore grudges, made threats.

Which concludes, Harriet told us, that behaviours like this could only have been side-effects of hunger. We in the group could stop wasting our time worrying that we needed to fix our relationships with our mothers, with our thighs, with adulthood, with men, or whatever it was that kept us awake. *These* were men! Harriet might as well have shrieked. Their relationships with their mothers were *fine!* They were obviously mature, at peace with their thighs, at peace with all the world. To Harriet's mind, all these men had in common with the women in my group were the biological effects of starvation. Whatever it was that had caused us to dig our hunger holes – in our case an anorexic 'personality type'; in theirs, a commitment to science – the thing that kept us sick was the same: nothing more than a suboptimal measure of potatoes. Fix that, she said, and you, like all those men, will get better again.

Keys's study has resonated widely in an era of neurobiological science – a time more interested in the brain, starved or otherwise, than the rather more nebulous mind. To think of mental illness this way – as biologically contained – suits a treatment model grounded in rapid, cheap, simplified solutions. If an anorexic patient starts to take up time by expressing opinions about her reluctance to eat, she must now contend with 1,385 pages of evidence against her in the form of Keys's book, *The Biology of Human Starvation*. Citing the insights of the Minnesota study, modern researchers advise that 'trying to make meaningful psychological changes with an anorexic patient in [a] starved state' is 'analogous to trying to investigate the underlying issues with an alcoholic patient who is intoxicated'. 'Your brains', Harriet informed us, 'have shrunken in size. Eat first, then see what you think.' What began as a guide to rebuilding strength for victims of famine and prisoners of war, has since come to justify clinicians' casual dismissal of anorexic personhood.

Chomping my sandwich several months later, I wondered how Harriet *knew* that those men had been so OK. That nothing they said, suffered or did could be interpreted other than through the lens of physical depletion. This may have been Keys's framework, but Keys had never been looking for anything other than the effects of a biological process; a process of starvation that he oversaw himself and treated as entirely neutral. But can you imagine a neutral experience of starving, either in or outside the scientist's lab? It is true that the Minnesota men's 'anorexic' careers had not begun with any objection to food. But should we therefore assume that these men objected to nothing at all?

In the first instance, at least, they had objected to the war. Which is to say, the thirty-six men used for the study had been drawn from a pool of conscientious objectors. COs in the Second World War were assigned to the Civilian Public Service (CPS), a programme that gave them useful things to do that didn't involve taking up arms.

Even with the CPS, it wasn't easy for these men to do the kinds of work they wanted. In the eyes of a disapproving public, men such as these were unfit to be redeemed through public service. In 1942, the government briefly aired the prospect of sending COs to perform relief work overseas, but Congressmen blocked the opportunity, appalled that 'slackers' like these would have a chance to be made to feel brave. The War Department appropriation bill of January 1943 prohibited the use of government money for sending CPS men abroad. CPS men despaired at this. They were desperate for something to do. They objected to the ways in which society at large tried to keep them from fulfilling their ideals.

Keys's research team were keenly aware of the depth of this desperation. It seems there was a lot these men would suffer short of blowing out other men's brains, particularly for medical science. Some signed up to gargle sputa from pneumonia-infected lungs, clasped boxes of malarial mosquitos to their bellies. Others put on lice-infested underpants with the aim of picking up typhus. Then there were the hundreds who applied to take part in Keys's starvation experiment: an entire year surrendering all their dietary freedom, the first six months marked for wasting away on a diet of cabbage and peas.

When it came to recruiting volunteers, Keys and his associates pitched the starvation study as a route to moral salvation. Along with their full-time duty of hunger – a public service in itself – the men would be offered free university tuition and enrolment in a 'school of foreign relief'. Here they would at least learn the skills required to do the kind of work they dreamt of. In the meantime, the study's recruitment pamphlet, written by another CO who was working on Keys's team, addressed fellow CPS men directly: 'Every avenue of relief service has been closed to us, but here's something we can now do.' On the cover were three small children closely examining empty bowls, beneath them the words: 'WILL YOU *STARVE* THAT *THEY* BE BETTER FED?'

This equation was more than mere rhetoric; the need to 'better' feed others was evidently urgent. Continental Europe relied on food imports even in peacetime, and not only had the region been under fire since 1939, but so had the usual shipping of foodstuffs been disrupted by naval warfare. US newspapers routinely reported on the food crisis, particularly in France – abject scenes of mass tubercular death, an imminent potential for riot.

The Minnesota men had reason to believe in a point to their starvation – a well-defined social utility for every moment of hunger. What's more, the final thirty-six participants had been carefully chosen for their tendency to care about these things. Among the selection criteria were a 'willingness to subordinate personal interests, activities and welfare to the requirements of the experimental program', and 'active interest in the problems of nutritional relief and rehabilitation'.

If you believe that difficulties with eating, or in fact any kind of mental struggle, stem from nothing more than hard-wired personality types, the Minnesota men – or at least to today's researchers – certainly fit a different profile from the one that is drawn for anorexics. Anorexics, according to the Maudsley model of treatment I have described, are anxious, introspective, emotionally and socially impaired. The Minnesota men, by contrast, were thoroughly outward-looking, civic-minded. Perhaps it is no wonder that the Harriets of this world, whose living is made off Maudsley's wisdom, are so quick to look at these men and see only their empty stomachs. If the only explanations for strange behaviour, to your mind, are biological – type of brain or state of body – to rule out 'type of brain' is to leave yourself with only one thing left to see.

But if you are willing to consider that our relationship with food might grow from more than biological factors, you are likely to find a lot more in the tale of the Minnesota men. While you may never be able to say with cold authority why the men became so strange – so fantastically obsessed with how they ate – you will see a much wider range of possible explanations. The Minnesota men, for example, were not just civic-minded by nature; they were disempowered actors in a literal world war. Their sense of civic purpose was not just innate – it was both socially contingent and fragile.

It is true that when the study began, the men showed some pretty high spirits. At this time, they ate their meals together in the football stadium of the University of Minnesota, the campus of which became their home for the duration of the study. For the first twelve weeks they reported themselves well fed and energetic. They volunteered in local settlement houses, acted in local plays, played instruments in town, organised dances, went to concerts, dated women, lived lives. And it is true that it was only when the study progressed into semi-starvation stage that their moods began to go south. A shock to their calorific intake, designed to mimic the siege of Leningrad, coincided with the first significant dent in the Minnesota men's missionary zeal.

Keys concluded that the men's good moods were directly proportional to their good diets. Yet their calorific intake was not the only variable at play. Their psychological decline could also have been linked with events that cast the very value of the experiment into doubt. Only a few months in, the war began to conclude. The need to start implementing relief plans came more quickly into view than expected. The results of the experiment, it seemed, would never be ready on time. Indeed, the war ended before the study's test subjects had been re-fed – the whole point of all their starvation. Allied relief efforts in Europe and Asia would have to forge ahead without the benefit of Keys's findings. Doctors around the world would have to speculate as to the merits of vitamins, protein percentages and feeding tubes.

This did not, by itself, completely deflate the Minnesota men. They forged ahead, gripping onto their hope that the work would at least be useful for *some*. But this was not the end of their demoralisation by external factors. The study itself gave plenty for the men to feel shitty about.

I am not talking, here, merely about the amount of food these men ate. This was exactly, after all, what they signed up for. I am talking about the stunningly dehumanising way in which their eating was observed and controlled. Keys enforced the strict limitation of quantities with humiliating suspicion. Mid-way through the starvation phase, he introduced a buddy system so the men could police one another. The result, perhaps predictably, was mutual resentment, irritation and wounded pride. When one of the men was caught eating in secret, Keys's response was to double down – each man would now be surveilled round the clock by one of the others. If you didn't have a buddy to go with you to a class, or to church, then God and education could wait. No one was prepared to go dating with a buddy in tow, so from that point on, the men were chaste.

In an atmosphere of such scrutiny and mutual mistrust, even the closest buddy will make a man feel more alone. Nothing in that study was designed to nurture solidarity in starvation. From the start, each participant's dietary ordeal was carefully individualised, the amount of food he received depending on how well he was descending towards his weekly target weight. Every Friday, a list of the participants would be posted, showing their rations for the following week. Additions and subtractions to the baseline diet were made in slices of bread. Like schoolkids divided in dignity with grades and gold stars, the men were classed by the calories they had earned with their weight-loss progress.

Though these were men whose decision to starve instead of going to war had been born of deeply pacifist principles, by a few months in, their interest in politics had been all but engulfed by thoughts about food. When Norman Mattoon Thomas, a five-time Socialist presidential candidate and celebrated advocate for nonviolence, came to give a lecture for the volunteers, they struggled to stay awake or ask the man anything that wasn't somehow about eating. When the war in Europe ended in May 1945, not one of the Minnesota men made any mention of it in his journal. All they wrote down were their changing body weights, reflections on meals, notes on the canteen queue.

Participant 20, Samuel Legg, had at the start of the study been typically idealistic. 'Everyone else was pulling down the world,' he reflected in an interview years later. 'We wanted to build it up.' All he wanted, like his fellow CPS members, was what they called 'significant work'. Halfway through the trial, he forgot all of this and began collecting cookbooks.

Legg began to eat in solitary silence, right at the end of the table. He began to play with his food – to heap the assortment of measly items on his plate into a single, hideous pile. Fish, peas, spaghetti and potatoes were smushed and stirred into a grey-green mass, encrusted with salt and pepper – two things he could use as much as he liked.

For where do you go when you find that your capacity to act has been all but reduced to pepper? Maybe you do resort to sculpting the materials to hand   fish, peas, spaghetti, potatoes. *Nowhere to go but inward* for the Minnesota men. Nowhere to channel all that energy but their bodies and their food.

Keys's regime of isolation showed no signs of abating when the time to refeed rolled round. The men, near deranged by their experience at this point, were divided into four different groups, each entitled to significantly different calorie counts. Legg was one of those unfortunate enough to land the fewest calories per day. Three weeks into refeeding, he silently left the canteen, went outside the building and chopped off three of his fingers.

This didn't stop Legg from begging Keys to let him complete the study. The moment he came round from his state of post-mutilation unconsciousness, he started making the case for why he had to keep going. 'For the rest of my life,' he gasped, 'people are going to ask what I did during the war. This experiment is my chance to give an honourable answer to that question.'

Perhaps he was right – maybe Ancel Keys's starvation experiment was an honourable gift to the world, whether or not its results were delayed; whether or not they came at the cost of three fingers and thirty-six wills to live. To the extent that Legg felt this, his decision to embark on the study must be distinguished from the average person's decision to embark on a weight-loss diet. But does this mean that Samuel Legg and an anorexic woman could have nothing in common but underfed brains? Nothing in common, for example, in their impotent desperation?

Medical researchers' reluctance to overidentify anorexic girls with politically minded heroes may have some shared features with feminists' reluctance to politicise the disease. In both cases, those who recoil from the comparison are right to shrink from the notion that refusing to eat is, by itself, a heroic thing to do. When feminists lament that the anorexic is read as 'rebellious and selfless', critiquing their comparison to saints, suffragettes and other political actors, they are right, at least, to reject the reduction of the condition to a personal disposition. What's more, when it comes to the *action* – the actual non-eating – they are right to query its rebellious impact. When Lisa Appignanesi casts anorexic girls as 'suicide bombers inside the bourgeois nuclear family', we sense, by juxtaposition, the gap between the organised martyr and the chaotic private drama of illness: one declares war on an entire set of values, the other on one's mere inner circle.

Yet to refuse the search for resonance in the historical record of hunger is to shed a load of other things too. An interest, for example, in where suffragettes and saints both sat in a matrix of power. A medieval saint is not interesting for her moral status alone. What if other aspects of a fasting nun's life could illuminate other kinds of suffering? What would it mean not to throw the baby of curiosity out with the bathwater of lazy analogy? What would it mean to stick with comparison of different kinds of starvation, not to rank or certificate them morally, but simply to *historicise*?

When I think of Samuel Legg, three fingers to the wind, pleading with Keys to let him starve, I think of the mystic philosopher and sometime-activist Simone Weil. Two years before the finger incident, Weil had starved herself to death. A year before that, she had been pleading with the general Charles de Gaulle to give *her* a sense of purpose in the war.

First a middle-class schoolteacher in France, who gave most of her wages to a strike fund; then a factory worker and author of *La condition ouvrière* – a text on the crushing effects of capitalist labour – Simone Weil was a master of trying, and often failing, to do things other people didn't want her to do. Mostly, this involved trying to share in the suffering of those less well-heeled than herself. In her work on assembly lines she was bullied by the foremen, fired, made redundant, fired again. In 1936, after securing herself a volunteer role in the Spanish Civil War, she managed to persuade her higher ups that she wasn't so short sighted (she was) that she couldn't be trusted with a rifle. The adventure was still cut short when she stepped in a vat of boiling oil, sprouting blisters on her vision of public service.

By 1942, Weil was languishing with her family in New York. They had just outpaced the German invasion of Paris, her hometown, where people were hungry. Weil had had the idea of organising volunteer Allied nurses to go and spend time on the frontlines. She'd hoped that someone in New York would get behind the idea. When it seemed that this was not going to happen, she petitioned to join the shadow Free French government, led by de Gaulle in London. Though she made it there, he too assumed she was joking about the nurses, so instead she begged to be sent to join the French Resistance in Paris. 'I confess', she wrote to her friend and comrade in spirit Maurice Schumann, 'that I can hardly bear to contemplate the thought of not being allowed to go.' This would be the final disappointment that she would, in fact, bear. She would spend the remaining months of her life consigned by the Free French government to bureaucratic admin.

It was then, trapped in London editing memoranda, that Weil stopped eating much at all. When in April 1943 she was admitted to Middlesex Hospital, she claimed to be rationing her food intake in solidarity with her compatriots. This was not the kind of organised hunger strike that was taking place elsewhere. The month before Weil went into hospital, Gandhi had been fasting for twenty-one days in connection with the Bengal famine, after the British had let market forces ravage the Indian food supply. The viceroy wanted Gandhi to admit that the Indians themselves were responsible for unrest in the region. Rather than simply refusing, Gandhi also refused to eat. Gandhi believed that there was spiritual value in hunger – that abstinence could set the soul free. But he also meant to put pressure on the levers of power, to push the cause of Indian freedom from British rule.

When Weil died in an Ashford sanitorium in August 1943, her fast had likely put pressure on nothing but her insides. As the physician who recorded her death put it, she had simply 'killed and slain herself by refusing to eat'.

Weil's vision of solidaristic action had not always been so narrow. At university, her political horizons had included an end to the kind of class inequality that breeds mass starvation in the first place. She scolded her academic rival Simone de Beauvoir for suggesting the political priority should be *existential* nourishment. 'It's easy to see', she said to the other Simone, 'you've never gone hungry.' Her first book had been an analysis of Marxist thought, published under the title *Oppression and Liberty*. There had been a time when Weil chewed energetically on the dynamics of social change.

How could such a person come to believe that solidarity meant quietly starving to death? 'I cannot eat the bread of the English', Weil wrote to Schumann, 'without taking part in their war effort.' She couldn't take part in the war, so she couldn't take part in anything. Rather than *starving so that others be better fed*, Weil seemed to starve without a plan. She starved in a state of resignation. She starved in a way that looked more like chopping off your fingers when you're just about done with 'significant work'.

Weil had once thought of bread as fundamental to feeding the working-class struggle. After her stint in the early 1930s working in factories, witnessing the crushing effects of the profit imperative, Weil struggled to agree with Marx that it was possible for working people to 'make their own history' through revolution. Marx, she thought, had misunderstood the realities of class – the brute fact that workers, who used all their energy to survive, were utterly lacking in power. This was a woman who had tried her best to improve the conditions of workers, only to judge this an impossible task. Towards the start of the Second World War, she mused that workers needed poetry, not bread. 'They need that their life should be a poem.'

In her later years, Weil seemed to think of progress less in terms of revolution than a kind of spiritual transcendence. 'The transcendent bread', she wrote in 1942, 'is the bread of today.' Perhaps it didn't matter, she thought, if you couldn't fill everyone's stomach with actual bread, since in the end only God could fill the 'void' within. In fact, perhaps it was better to leave the belly empty – leave a little room for God. 'All the desire which nature has placed in the human soul and attached to food,' she wrote, 'should be detached from [such] things and directed exclusively towards obedience to God.' If she could please God by being hungry, went the logic, maybe everyone would be saved. 'Ask that God may transform our flesh into Christ's flesh,' she advised, 'so that we may be food for all the afflicted.'

Claims like this have long been categorised as acts of conscious will – as chosen forms of protest. For historian Rudolph Bell, it was righteous indignation that had the 'holy anorexics' of medieval Italy wreaking havoc on their own bodies. Between the thirteenth and seventeenth centuries, clusters of nuns, according to Bell, 'decided' to starve on spiritual grounds. Religion provided a framework for escape from a world where the body was a site of corruption.

Women's bodies, in particular, faced constant invasion – from penises, from food, from any number of other pollutants. But a woman could 'decide with no small amount of pressure from catechism lessons only she takes literally and seriously', that the noblest response was to refuse. 'The holy anorexic', writes Bell, 'rebels against the passive, vicarious, dependent Christianity; her piety centers intensely and personally upon Jesus and his crucifixion, and she actively seeks an intimate, physical union with God.'

So off she goes, refusing food and eating spiders instead; drinking water infused with lepers' putrefying flesh. Gathering pus from cancerous sores into ladles and drinking it down 'to overcome all bodily sensations'. When Catherine of Siena had finished with her ladle, she dreamt of Jesus inviting her to drink from his wounds. Her stomach, in that moment, reportedly 'no longer had need of food'. For Bell, the holy anorexic's total dependence on God's will 'legitimises her defiance and places her in a position of enormous strength'. I suppose that really depends on how you think about strength. How you think about choice, about power.

For in an ideal world, should a woman really need to eat spiders to feel strong? Is this the kind of power she would choose for herself if other kinds of power were available? Would this kind of union with Jesus have tasted so good had it not felt quite so urgent, for example, to escape the forced union of marriage? This is not to deny the idea that self-starvation gave these women a kind of psychological strength – that it provided a sense of autonomy in a patriarchal world. But this is not the same as giving them the power to change the patriarchal order.

It is difficult to believe that in an ideal world, Simone Weil would have wanted the poor to live on poems. Even in her dying months, she kept one foot in a fantasy of herself as a person she considered worth feeding. The letters she wrote to her parents from London spent no time trying to elevate the agony of an empty stomach. Instead, they represent fantasies of a Simone who ate gladly, who considered it noble to eat. She reports on the happy surprise of finding some traditional English food – roast lamb and mint sauce – 'remarkable'. Roast pork, too, with apple sauce she declares an 'honourable' dish. 'The pure taste of the apples is as much a contact with the beauty of the universe as the contemplation of a picture by Cézanne.' She complains that English pubs tend not to serve food – how is she supposed to keep down her stout?

The regime of abstinence the real Simone was imposing on herself was at odds not only with that fantasy but with the ideals she harboured for her parents. Her notebooks from her dying years – private repositories of doom – speak of pleasure as nothing but an illusion. It was an illusion, she wrote, to believe that there was any good to human existence. With that in mind, she aspired to experience 'an excess of physical suffering', and not to forget the lessons it taught. Yet in her letters she seems genuinely moved by the concern that her parents can't afford nice things. 'Do please tell me the truth,' she insists. 'A little pleasure is necessary in this world, like bread and water (or Coca-Cola and cornflakes).'

Which Weil was right? The one who believed in cornflakes, or the one who thought their pleasures were elusive? The Weil who saw a point to feeding oneself, or the one who considered eating a lost cause? It is hard to adjudicate how hopeful one should be about the world. In the end, we can to some extent only hope that hope is a thing worth having.

For the purposes of eating my sandwich, I preferred to imagine that Weil had been wrong about Marx. Weil considered the working class a fundamentally downtrodden people – a factually powerless group. Marx, on the other hand, thought of class as more of a project than a fact – a process of coming to understand yourself a certain way. If the working class did not yet have the power to start a revolution, this was because they had not yet been *empowered*. And what could be less empowering than thinking of yourself as a person who doesn't need bread? What would it take to inspire those people who literally couldn't get food to consider bread and cornflakes their right? Probably not the spiritual fasts of middle-class philosopher-writers.

Solidarity requires not just the recognition of a shared political enemy, but the collectively generated sense that the enemy can be beaten. This process of coming into power is starkly played out in the story of Marx's own daughter. It goes without saying that without Karl Marx, there would be no Marxist feminism – broadly, a social movement that links the subjugation of women with the upkeep of patriarchal capitalism. Unfortunately, Marx himself was guilty of certain patriarchal manoeuvres, at least within the confines of his own (nuclear) household.

The defeat of the Paris commune in 1871, when Eleanor Marx was sixteen years old, had filled the Marx family household in London with French political refugees. One of the most prominent among them, named Hippolyte Lissagaray, became the young Eleanor's boyfriend. Her father Karl did not approve.

As Karl became increasingly demanding of his daughter's attention, insisting she assist with his research, Eleanor took it upon herself to make her way out. She found herself a teaching job in Brighton and took her love of politics there. She buoyed herself up by introducing young people to the international labour movement.

According to Rachel Holmes's biography of Eleanor Marx, her appetite then was pretty healthy. On Lissagaray's weekend visits, the pair would take seafront walks. As they deconstructed politics and debated the future direction of class struggle, they did so with mouths full of fish and chips, eels, clams and whelks. They 'rambled', writes Holmes, 'over the Sussex downs with picnics of bread, cheese and wine . . . ending the day in lamplit country pubs with pies and pints of ale.'

But Eleanor wasn't always able to eat exactly as she chose. Food was frequently thrust on her unwanted. It is said that Karl, in childhood, was prone to making his sisters swallow down mud pies. It seems as though perhaps his wife Jenny got her kicks from similar places. While Eleanor makes no mention of her health in any letters to her parents, Jenny's missives address her daughter as though she were always on the brink of starvation. She is reported to have sent Eleanor endless chocolates, along with parcels of potted meat, fretting that Brighton's food might be too rough for her delicate child. Her letters are stuffed with injunctions not to swim too long, not to take on too many pupils, spend too much time in thought.

Eventually, Eleanor's parents demanded she come back home. It wasn't that they had heard any hint of illness or distress. Instead, the thing that bothered them was that people in Brighton had been saying that Eleanor was engaged. This would have given her the freedom to walk around unchaperoned with her boyfriend, a freedom too extreme for Karl and Jenny. Eleanor at first resisted the call, but her parents got her in the end. She bent to their will, left her job, went home, and found she could no longer eat.

Eleanor's doctor in 1874 was Elizabeth Garrett Anderson, a suffragist and the first British woman to qualify as a physician. Unlike many eating disorders specialists today, who objectify their patients as stomachs to be filled before they can be dealt with as people, Garrett Anderson saw a need for Eleanor *both* to be nourished *and* afforded a sense of purpose. She saw the ways that Eleanor's parents had overwhelmed her developing values, reducing her life from one of teaching, debate and a mind-expanding romance to one of daughterly admin and asphyxiating surveillance. She tactfully advised that the Marxes focus on getting their daughter fed, while also ensuring her exposure, in the process, to a world outside.

Karl reported that the family's encouragement improved her diet 'in geometric proportions'. But from Eleanor's own correspondence, it seems that other factors were also at play. As part of Garrett Anderson's prescription, Eleanor went on a retreat with her father to Karlsbad forest and spa in Austria. At Karlsbad, she certainly ate and enjoyed the local pilsner, but she also did so in the company of garrulous writers and artists, fellow radicals in exile, people who excited her appetite. A person isn't inspired to start eating again by nothing more than other people's advice. In Austria, Eleanor ate among people who nourished her ideas, and likely nourished her reason to eat.

On the way back, she and Karl went to Leipzig and visited the family of Wilhelm Liebknecht, one of the first founders of the German Social Democratic Party. Wilhelm listened generously to Eleanor's grief about her parents' distaste for her relationship, while also giving her other things to think about instead. The two of them began to work together coordinating socialist efforts in Germany and France. This, according to Holmes, was a turning point for Eleanor, 'depression overcome, appetite regained, engaged in matters of the world at large'.

Eleanor, unlike Weil, found it in her to eat again, and unlike Weil found it in her to hope. Of course, this still cannot tell us whether hope of this kind is actually a thing worth having. More instructive in that regard are the details of where Eleanor's enthusiasm took her. Not just whether she ate, but what this allowed her to imagine and achieve.

Eleanor, like Weil, had been fortunate enough to be able to afford to eat. They had also both been free to eat, in the most basic sense, in that they lived outside of prison conditions. The privileged context for their hunger set them apart from many other hungry people. Yet Eleanor's growing consciousness of the ways in which women also suffered a species of imprisonment, a species of dispossession, bolstered her sense of solidarity with subjugated people quite different from herself. This solidarity was not merely nominal – an empty expression of allegiance. After Eleanor returned to life and resumed her relationship with Lissagaray, she turned towards a range of anti-imperialist struggles. Specifically, she turned her energies against the English use of hunger as a weapon.

Eleanor's writings on the persecution of the Irish bear witness to the depth of her political feeling. In this, she resembled her father, who had already written on the English control of Irish eating in his critique of the industrial-capitalist food system. British agriculture, he observed, was an imperial system. The soil fertility crisis of the 1830s and 40s saw fertiliser exported from Ireland to England, with the Irish receiving little or nothing back. The shift from cereal and grain production to livestock and forage-crop farming meant more food for the upper classes, but a lot less bread for everyone else. Meat-based agriculture also needed far fewer workers, meaning the displacement, between 1855 and 1866, of over a million Irish men by cattle, pigs and sheep. The cost of colonial profit, Marx observed, was widespread Irish hunger. Some twenty years later, Eleanor's challenge to the cost of colonial violence focused on the starving of Irish political prisoners.

In 1884, Eleanor authored a number of tracts inciting sympathy with the Irish Dynamiters – a group of Irish-Americans committed to physically forcing a republic through bombing campaigns. Between 1881 and 1990, targets included the detective headquarters of the Dublin Metropolitan Police, Whitehall, Scotland Yard and the chamber of the House of Commons. Without suggesting that violence of this order could ever be politically productive, Eleanor wrote of the importance of understanding the campaign not as an act of unexplained evil, but a response to systematic oppression. The bombings seemed to Eleanor nothing less than what can happen when you persecute a whole population, subjecting its people to the disfigurations and desperation of hunger. When you have been or are being starved, Eleanor saw, conditions aren't ideal for strategising slow political action. In fact, the effects of forced hunger could literally be explosive.

In one of these tracts, Eleanor takes up the case of an Irish republican man imprisoned for refusing to declare his religion, prior to his bombing career. She describes in revolting detail the penal diet to which he was subjected. Even the 'normal' diet for men in these prisons was of a quantity so small that 'a child could scarcely live on it'. Additional penal flourishes included garnishing these scraps with 'untanned skin', hair and, apparently, snails. Prisoners were reported to be eating candles and soap, and drinking the oil meant for boots. If the man was now a terrorist, Eleanor wrote, his crimes were in part the metabolised product of state brutal-isation. Whatever his crimes, she wrote, 'there is a greater criminal than he – the English Government, that has made him what he is'.

The line between how a person eats and how they under-stand the world can never be straight or clear, but can we deny that it is there? Any more than we can deny the con-nection between how a person understands the world and the mark they leave upon it? To strengthen oneself with food can be empowering; to be cajoled into eating overwhelming. A hunger strike can bring about political change; forced star-vation can bring about bombs. What might the men who became the Irish Dynamiters have done with themselves had they not been debased by a diet of soap and snails? How much less might Eleanor Marx have achieved had she forever been force-fed potted meat by her parents? Ancel Keys's writing on the biology of starvation can only tell us so much. It can tell us what happens to a hungry body and brain, while saying nothing of the mind or the soul.

I have come to believe that the greatest value of Keys's study when it comes to thinking about starvation lies not in its 'findings', but in the story that gave rise to them. To me, the most revelatory moment in the tale of the Minnesota men takes place in week twenty-seven, when, anxious about morale among his lab rats, Keys permitted them a single 'relief meal'. On this one occasion, the men were allowed to contribute to the menu themselves, and to eat it together, each man receiving the same as everyone else. Craving grease and bulk, they went for bacon, eggs and biscuits, but they also made more whimsical choices – peanut butter, grape-fruit juice, strawberries, fruit punch. Meat could now have gravy, bread could have butter and honey. Food was not just about weight control; it was something to be savoured and embellished.

When the meal came round, a group of men who had learnt to suspect and resent one another were able to laugh while eating, for the first time in months. They ate together companionably, remembered the shared ambition that had brought them there in the first place. And though Keys had tried to regulate every calorie in the feast, they found them-selves a way to confound him. Emboldened by their long-lost sense of autonomy, they also ate the peel of every orange.

Even on Keys's terms, calories alone could not account for this radical change of behaviour. According to the logic of *The Biology of Human Starvation*, and indeed of modern eating disorder treatments, a person has to gain significant weight before meaningful psychological changes can be seen. To exit the clinical 'starvation state', you must achieve a clinically respectable BMI. Yet the Minnesota men transformed for a day without the need for sustained, controlled refeeding. And by contrast, the first weeks of refeeding were far from a time of calorie-induced bliss. As we have seen, they were in fact a time of terrible angst and severed fingers. Though according to Keys, the pace of recovery from starvation is related *only* to the level of calories consumed, accounts of the story behind his study suggest that context was just as important.

It wasn't until September 1945 that things really began to change. It was only then, quite a way into refeeding, that Keys gave every man an extra 800 calories per day. It was also only then that the men could graduate from two meals a day to the socially customary three. At last, their bread was dignified with butter and jam. At last, the men were reacquainted with sweet potatoes. Though it still took a while for them to gain any weight, their spirits began to soar. Only two days into this new way of life, the men began to organise together. It only took a few good meals, eaten with equal dignity and entitlement, to spur the men to devise a set of demands to present to Keys. They typed a manifesto, threatening non-cooperation in the study if he didn't take note. The first of these demands was for the abolition of the buddy system.

This micro-radicalisation – a small but successful moment of collective bargaining – was only the beginning for the Minnesota men of a return to political consciousness. After the study was over, ten of the men would go on to work in international relief efforts, while others ran for office or lectured on hunger and its global significance. Samuel Legg joined the American Friends Service Committee, raising money to send food to Europe. He later became entangled in the struggle against the Vietnam War. For the rest of his life, he found the energy to keep causing trouble with the police. At eighty-two years old, he was arrested for protesting the bombing of Yugoslavia.

These men had not been able to save themselves from helplessness through elaborate salt and pepper rituals any more than Catherine of Siena was able to transform the patriarchy by drinking pus from cancerous sores. Anorexia and its routines can offer a sense of control, but this should not be mistaken for power. Yet nor had food alone – the mere re-injection of calorific substances – been enough to restore these men to a belief in their own capacities. As with Eleanor Marx, it took a certain confluence of food, conviviality and respect.

What if the things that complicate sandwiches – the feelings they inspire – encompass more than their calorific content? More, in fact, than all the details of their contents and what we think those contents mean. There I was looking at bread and wondering if liking it made me 'normal', whether it changed my diagnosis, whether it made me look down-to-earth. I had never really considered the things that mattered, sandwich-wise – not the things you scrutinise to tell you what you are, but the things that go to shape how you feel about the world. Like whether your sandwich is one of those miserable single-layer cheese ones the UK government thought would be good enough for hungry children in the pandemic; like whether your sandwich has been designed in a spirit of indifference and budgeted for in a spirit of contempt. Or whether your sandwich has been abstracted into a beige liquid diet and pulsed through your nostrils via a tube because in fact, you do not want to eat a sandwich; you are not sure you ever want to eat again.

Or whether your sandwich represents an attempt at life – at giving yourself a chance. If it has been made by someone who thinks about whether or not you like pickles. If you made it for yourself and made it well. If you have been given the time to eat it by a society that believes in lunch breaks, and assumes that people should be fed. The sandwich has a history of holding both people and protein in its embrace, yet I held my own in such profound suspicion.

I needed some kind of relief meal – one that might raise my spirits high enough to make me want to eat a whole lemon. I needed inspiration to eat in ways that might spare me a fate like Weil's. Restricting her food (A); of a very low weight (B); resistant to reversing this trajectory (C); but also a great deal more besides: out of love with the dream of revolution.

2

You Restrict

One man's relief can be another man's torment. If I thought about the meals I'd eaten that had already gone down easier than others, they bore very little resemblance to the feast of the Minnesota men. Those men had found strength in chicken, in bacon and ham. These were foods that gave me especially difficult feelings.

When I began to seek out a relief meal after that clinical trial, the most relief I had recently felt had been in food that had never had a nervous system. If I was going to eat at all, I'd do it the way I'd been doing it for years: I'd take my pasta with mushrooms rather than meat, olive oil instead of rendered nubs of fat. But I knew that what for me was an indulgence could also be another man's restriction. However fatty, smoky, chewy, even 'meaty' this diet could have been, there would always be a majority who heard the word 'vegan' and sensed a kind of dietary fascism. With that in mind, any relief I might have found in avoiding meat was cut with a dose of unease.

Why, you might not be wondering, would a society wish to frame a meatless diet this way? I myself had never wondered such a thing until this point, simply wearing the requisite shame. It wasn't until my own veganism began to intersect with a restriction yet more shameful that the edifice of shame began to wobble. That I began to question the nature of our cultural distaste for 'giving up' foods.

To be both vegan and anorexic is not, let's face it, an easy combination to defend. Anorexia alone is frequently construed as a totalitarian condition. Where earlier feminist theories saw the illness as a mere *reaction* to patriarchal authority – to the fascist hand of paternal or parental control – contemporary feminist thought casts the anorexic *herself* as the fascist actor. Or more accurately as both – as victim and villain at once. Having internalised a patriarchal command to be thin, she turns herself into the problem. However sexless her exaggerated 'beauty', she is held to be sleeping with the enemy.

Ubiquitous references to anorexic 'body fascism' still call on Naomi Wolf's 1990 bestseller *The Beauty Myth*, in which the one-time feminist intellectual compared the anorexic to the 'anti-Semitic Jew' and the 'self-hating black'. Though Wolf was strongly of the opinion that the disease was not a choice, but rather a side effect of patriarchal beauty ideals, she still lamented the younger generation's weakness in the face of its temptations; she diagnosed in these women an 'inert relationship to feminism'. Forecasting a third wave of the movement 'frozen in motion' by obsessive under-fuelling, she warned that *women these days* were letting the other side win. To share a meal with a younger woman, Wolf complained, was to sit down to a kind of ideological warfare. The junior anorexic tyrannises you with her ice-cube-sucking, breadstick-hiding antics. You must either ignore her provocative behaviour, Wolf mused, or suffer her cold aggression.

Gone, for Wolf, were the sisterly 1960s and 70s, when women could be ugly and strong. In was the era of lobotomised Barbie dolls, wasting the one or two calories they ate on generating dinner table melodramas. In Todd Haynes's 1980s film *Superstar: The Karen Carpenter Story*, a melodrama acted out by Barbie dolls, celebrity pop duo Karen and Richard Carpenter battle over the dinner table. Barbie Karen (anorexic) is eating salad. Richard (normal) is eating meat. Karen complains that life on the road is draining her will to live. Richard retorts that this is what happens when you don't eat enough food. He tries to make Karen take a bite of his steak. She resists, becomes shrill, makes a scene. Everyone has a bad time thanks to Karen's belligerent ways.

The scene abruptly changes to a reel of supermarket aisles – shelves upon shelves of cheap abundance. Text cards, overlaid on this backdrop of boxes and cans, characterise Karen's disease as 'a fascism over the body in which the sufferer plays the part of both dictator and emaciated victim'. Her behaviour is both a resistance to American overconsumption – to the postwar frenzy in which 'few could leave the supermarket without buying more than they intended' – and an insult to American freedom, to the pleasures of joining in.

Today's biomedical wisdom keeps this element of paradox but abandons the traditional victim narratives. No more tales of the anorexic as subject to patriarchal control or conscription to a dark consumer culture. If the modern anorexic is a victim, she is a victim of bad genes. Her innate 'thinking styles' – rigid, rule-bound, blinkered – are in no real way her fault, but like all varieties of fascism, they must be stamped out. For the anorexic might not literally be a populist-nationalist actor in an organised political movement, but like her analogue, she shows a vexing disregard for the more reasonable perspectives of others. Like the fascist proper, she cleaves to tradition – traditions she has invented in her sad little nation of one. She seems to stand against pleasure, to want to subject the world, autocratically, to an embargo on fun. She is simply, when all attempts at analysis fail, an example of the worst.

Anorexics are considered, like fascists, to be so beyond the pale as to justify the use of force against them. Most medical models of treatment endorse the use of force-feeding, not only as a means of forestalling death, but also as a punishment for noncompliant behaviour. In the Maudsley model, until a patient has learnt to express themselves 'appropriately' and 'see the world from other people's perspective', they can expect to be submitted to a regime of intimate surveillance and intimidation. The 'care' manual given to my boyfriend when I embarked upon this treatment instructed him to sidestep any 'battles' I might begin by 'calling on a higher authority'. Examples he'd perform ironically in an attempt at dark humour included citing the NHS guidelines as a reason not to indulge me in conversations about food. He was offered impersonal-sounding threats to try out, like: 'If you choose not to eat now then it may be that many more freedoms will disappear with hospital treatment.' The idea was for me to fear this unfreedom enough that I'd learn to behave without external coercion. Mine was a treatment composed of mottoes taken straight from the panopticon: 'Integrity is doing the right thing when nobody is looking.'

One of the techniques through which carers are persuaded to treat the people they love this way is a framing of anorexics as possessed by a kind of sub-human other. This way, the fascist personality can be separated from the 'true' (potential) person within. 'Remember,' Matt was instructed by the guide, 'with anorexia it is as if an "anorexic minx" is sitting on the chair with the patient whispering critical and judgemental remarks.' The minx, he was given to understand, kept calling me a 'stupid, fat bitch'. I wondered, when I read this myself, if the people who wrote the guide had something to get off their chests. Neither 'stupid' nor 'fat' was a word I could imagine applying to myself; neither 'minx' nor 'bitch' compatible with my basic respect for women.

Still, I had come to accept the idea of myself as a little bit fascist. Could I really disagree that my behaviour was, more or less, the worst? I think it was a bit like coming to accept the idea that there is no God – disappointing, but hard to refute without a considerable investment of thought. Sometimes life is not conducive to the sense of a divine master plan. If you're anorexic, the discourse around you is not conducive to forming an optimistic impression of yourself.

If you are vegan, this kind of self-consciousness is heightened by another layer of cultural suspicion. Society at large, in my experience, does not hesitate to hate a vegan. If, for Anthony Bourdain, a vegetarian was 'the enemy of everything good and decent in the human spirit', the vegan continues to represent part of a 'Hezbollah-like splinter faction'. Protestors bait them at London markets by theatrically eating raw squirrels; reckless magazine editors are fired for proposing pieces on how to kill them. When an openly anorexic individual reveals themself to be vegan too, the wheels of speculation start turning as to which disease gave way to the other.

Reams of medical research are concerned with the high proportion of vegetarians among people with eating disorders. Though they cannot agree on a cause, the papers generally conclude by warning that a meat-free diet can serve to mask and maintain the symptoms of illness.

Nowhere is this warning taken more seriously than online journalism, where livings are made from a rapacious economy of catching people out. The *Independent* dubs anorexia 'The Dark Side of Veganism'. In outlets from the Huffington Post to the BBC, aspiring young writers with eating disorders are routinely commissioned to affirm this line of thought: 'My Vegan Diet Looked Healthful on the Outside', reads one such header, 'Here's What Nobody Knew'. Or, in more straight-talking versions, 'I Went Vegan to Hide My Eating Disorder'. These confessionals build their authority around truths universally acknowledged: that vegans exist to be discredited, and that anorexics are liars. Their aim is not to ask why anorexics might feel the need to lie, nor adjudicate the value of veganism beyond helping them to do it. The aim is to gather evidence for a more fundamental belief: that certain restrictions on diet pose a threat to the liberal order.

Until very recently, most eating disorder facilities refused to even accept vegan patients. For what is recovery from *dis*order, by these institutions' measures, if not submission to the prevailing order? *Seeing the world from other people's perspective* means wanting to be normal – fertile, productive, happy with your lot. An enthusiast of the diet that keeps our economy running – running on animal milk and meat.

It is easy, when such things are thought to define *being well*, to question any desires that appear to contradict them. It is even easier to question your own motives when the pressure comes from outside the medical field as well as within it. When I had first begun to seek help with my aversion to eating, friends – who had encouraged me to do so – had expressed concern that I wouldn't be able to make much progress on a vegan diet. Their scepticism called on me to defend the vegan cause right when the leg I had to stand on was its thinnest. It had never been particularly easy to convince those around me this was a reasonable way to eat. 'It's just chicken *stock*,' they would say. 'You'll eat anchovies, though.' 'You won't mind if I use a bit of butter.' Either they had forgotten that chickens were animals, or perhaps that stock was real, or else they were asking simply to remind me I was ruining their lives.

There can certainly be a kind of relief in doing things the regular way. Until I had stopped eating meat, about four years earlier, I had vaguely believed my omnivorous diet to be a mark of good health, good humour, feminist achievement. I felt some pride in being adept at roasting birds, sliding carefree fistfuls of butter under their unsuspecting skin. When I started seeing Matt, who was vegetarian, we both referred to this fact as his 'problem'. When he told me one New Year's Day that he intended to give up dairy too, I am sure I looked at him as though he were responsible for all the boredom in the world. For a time, I had very few qualms about continuing to claw at the crisp, spiced edges of a friend's spatchcocked chicken, or to keep my own dedicated carton of milk from a cow in the door of the fridge. It is easier, in impolite society, to eat without making a fuss. It is easier to want what is wanted for you.

Then there is also the fact that history offers us grounds for linking dietary restriction with literal fascism. In the early twentieth century – the time of European dictatorships – some of the first signs of vegetarian trouble emerged from the Italian Regency of Carnaro. In 1919, part-time poet and part-time power-grabber Gabriele D'Annunzio led a group of Italian citizens to invade the disputed territory of Fiume (now Rijeka in Croatia) on the grounds that the Italian government didn't have the energy or strength. Italians, D'Annunzio thought, were far too stuffed with *adipe e grasseza* (fat and fatness) to win the region from Yugoslav hands.

Every day, D'Annunzio insisted, Italy's gluttonous prime minister Francesco Nitti was having to punch an extra hole in his belt, too concerned was he with mealtimes, not enough with domination. The poet is said to have pointedly installed a dead turtle on his dining table – a turtle who had supposedly gorged himself to death on roses in a fit of greedy flamboyance. The idea was for the turtle to serve as a cautionary tale for guests – an instruction to rein those Italian appetites in. His aim was to build a new regime on slim, dynamic men. His collaborator Guido Keller advised that these men should give up meat.

Vegetarianism, in Fiume, was supposedly a way of detoxing the soul, of purifying a nation corrupted by money and sex. While aspects of the Regency's politics were unarguably progressive – votes for women! care for the earth! free love! – there is certainly a proto-fascist flavour to the group's purity discourse, which linked the prime minister's gullet with the purported avarice of Jews. True to the group's undemocratic pursuit of authority, Keller cultivated something like a cult, persuading his followers to stop eating meat and to live off vegetables and honey. Eating, for Keller, was merely an unfortunate obligation. Sleeping in trees in a rented field, he made entire meals out of nothing but the fruit that was to hand.

If you really want to know about antisemitic vegetarian propaganda, you need of course look no further than the Nazis. Hitler's ideas about what made a man pure drew in part on the idea, borrowed from Wagner, that animal flesh was a source of contamination. Hitler's blood, body and mind, in the Nazi imagination, were as clear of animal protein as of booze and sexual thoughts. Jewish people, on the other hand, were almost-cannibalistic gobblers of meat. The Nazis may have been fine with the slaughter of Jews themselves, but Kosher slaughter was uniquely out of the question.

Of course, it was only a certain fantasy of meat that was important to the Nazis – not so much the fact of meat itself. They cared about its potential as a signifier of dirt, but not its status as actual animal flesh. Perhaps this accounts for why Hitler, though vegetarian in brand, was perfectly happy to fill up on liver, ham and game in moments off from making a point. When the Nazis got very into drugs, and Hitler's doctors were plying him with daily injections, he was also perfectly happy for these injections to contain a derivative of bull's testicles.

This kind of use of a vegetable diet as proof of divine superiority – a flimsy but relentless attempt to legitimate absolute power – recurs throughout fascist history like raw garlic in Mussolini's throat. Apparently, the dictator liked to eat this as a salad all of its own – another supposed path to perfection. Italian fascism proper was replete with magical thoughts about the meaning of diet, like the reframing of abject poverty as a patriotic gesture. Today, *cucina povera* – Italian 'pauper cuisine' – is a term often used by chefs to make poor-person food feel expensive. The Italian fascists used the term to rebrand food shortages as a source of national virtue. Turning simple food into a cultural tradition, it seems, took the edge off the fascist government's terrible foreign policy. In truth, fighting a war on the side of the Nazis and funnelling resources into imperialist expansion had stretched the nation so tightly you could barely get meat if you tried. How fortunate, then, that the style was to uphold a restricted diet as a matter of Italian honour. Cookbooks at the time listed the ingredients you *didn't* need for any given recipe – *niente pasta, niente riso, niente grassi* – nothing that nice.

Then there are also those historic veggies who thought themselves the enemies of fascism, but have since been fixed in the canon of patriarchal 'body fascists'. I am speaking of 'liberal' men, who might be credited with birthing the era of nutritional science, before the thought of meat as 'unclean' became a matter of industrial mass production. Before, that is, Upton Sinclair's 1906 novel *The Jungle* gave us the image of meat-packing plants as places where rats raced roughshod over germ-encrusted animal products. Nineteenth-century food reformers like John Harvey Kellogg (of cornflake fame) also built their names on pushing 'clean', unprocessed vegetarian diets as a matter of hygiene, but it was women's moral hygiene that preoccupied them most. In fact, for John Harvey and his brother Keith, the degenerate ways of meat-loving females were chief among the roots of societal disorder.

According to Kellogg's *Ladies' Guide in Health and Disease* (1892), 'stimulating' substances like meat not only weakened women's organs, but developed 'those parts of the system which would be better restrained'. Women's appetites were 'capricious' and needed to be regulated with grain-forward meal plans. It was a very great mistake, wrote Kellogg, for women to assume they needed mutton, beef-steak and eggs. Meat, along with pepper, vinegar and mustard, were mischievous diversions from the ladylike diet. Again, these recommendations have very little to do with what meat actually *is*. Kellogg's attack on meat consumption has little to do with animal slaughter and a lot to do with women's pleasure in food. 'A young lady who has ruined her digestion', Kellogg warned, 'does not want more meat but less knick-knacks. She does not require more beef-steak, but more oat-meal and less pastry.'

Accordingly, it was only the enjoyable kinds of meat that represented a problem for Kellogg. Like Hitler's doctors, he was happy enough to recommend animal products for self-improving, medicinal purposes. His list of Useful Dietetic Recipes, for example, includes a number of gruels, jellies and 'nutritive injections' made of animal meat and viscera. Beef-steak was forbidden, but pounded raw chicken simmered in water and passed through a sieve was fine. Better still was a 'solution' of pancreas and meat – or, alternatively, pancreas and cream – injected into the rectum. Shoot it up slowly, Kellogg advises, and if the anus won't comply, keep half in the fridge for later. Keep on shoving it in until the body behaves, as long as it gives you no pleasure.

Alongside the more misogynistic brand of vegetarian nutritional enterprise ran a liberal diet culture that considered itself progressive not just morally, but socially too. Even here, however, it is easy to identify traces of the body-fascist tendency.

The first organised vegetarians in England were certainly not all bad. Positing their cause as motivated by kindness, they affiliated themselves with movements that were kind to workers, kind to women, kind to animals used for science. In the mid nineteenth century, the British Vegetarian Society was connected with struggles for labour rights, women's suffrage and ending vivisection. American social reformers were inspired by all this, and added to the cluster of causes the emancipation of slaves.

Yet in the literatures produced by these groups, the strongest motivations still seem tied to the appearance of virtue. The American Vegetarian Society (AVS) was closely linked with the Temperance movement, founded by Bible Christians, and chief among its prized virtues was the virtue of abstention. This, according to the AVS, was the 'Archimedian lever of change' – the magical mechanism that made everything else OK, the thing that made people kind. At the Society's first formal meeting in 1851, it defined vegetarianism as an effort to bring about total reform through a prelapsarian diet. This diet was spiritually and morally clean, which meant being purified of meat. The lust for animal flesh, society members believed, was the kind of sadistic passion we'd been lumbered with by Eve. Humanity could only be saved through a repentant diet of plants.

A high-minded worship of asceticism rings through the record of the AVS. At an AVS 'banquet', you might be greeted by a bust of Milton, who warned in *Paradise Lost* that 'the lyrist may indulge in wine, and a free life, but he who would write an epic for the nations must eat beans and drink water'. The Society's *American Vegetarian and Health Journal* (*AVHJ*), published in the 1850s, is full of breathlessly learned references to the ancient Greeks, who apparently lived quite happily on just a few fruits, drinking nothing but the fluid that 'gushed and sparkled and danced' from mountains and springs. Advice columns warned that if parents wanted their children to 'live long and be intellectual', those parents would need to limit themselves to no more than two meals per day.

You would think a group that identified as socialist would also show an interest in more down-to-earth concerns. Yet not only do AVS writings show little evidence of interest in class struggle, their lofty tones are consistently underwritten by class hatred. If abstention from meat was both virtuous and refined, an appetite for animals was base, lumpen sin. *AVHJ* articles routinely remark on the dietary excess of the 'great mass', and the 'degradation' to which it has reduced them. An abolitionist, writing in the 1953 *Liberator* journal, compares a man whose stomach is 'crammed with animal abominations' to an alcoholic hobo, crusted over with dirt. Such people, he writes, 'can no more appreciate lofty moral and intellectual teachings than a swine can appreciate pearl necklaces. Logic, humor, pathos, eloquence, are wasted on such persons. Their gross habits block up every avenue by which sublime ideas might enter.'

You might also think that a group that positioned a dietary choice as 'feminist' might be concerned with women's dietary freedom. Instead, AVS rhetoric merely replaced women's servitude in the kitchen with their servitude to the rigours of clean eating. Frequent contributor J. H. Hanaford noted that 'woman, from an unjust demand of society – or *gluttony* – is incarcerated during so great a portion of her time'. Instead of the 'ceaseless odor of surloins, steams and hams', she should be out inhaling 'the sweet fragrance of myriads of flowers', breathing in the 'pure air of rural retreats' and frolicking in the beauty of creation. More to the point, she should herself avoid having to eat a substance so riddled with moral pestilence. For vegetarian educator Anne Denton, it was an affront to women's 'naturally refined and beautiful spirits' that they should have to partake of 'mangled flesh' – the pleasure of 'vitiated appetites'.

It is perhaps telling that as soon as social progress called for less-than-beautiful measures, the vegetarian movement fractured. When civil war broke out in 1861, those who were committed to the cause of abolishing slavery were ready to engage in violence. The AVS, however, was organised by a logic of virtue first, and social change second. Temperance, kindness and gentility were priorities for the group, rather than the socialism, feminism or abolitionism they purported to serve. Virtue as an end in itself, in other words, rather than a means to anything bigger. Some abolitionist members abandoned their anti-meat rhetoric at this point. The rest would need to find a new justification for themselves.

By the end of the nineteenth century, organised vegetarians tended to brand themselves more as health pioneers than social activists. The figureheads of the 'movement' were no longer socialists, abolitionists or feminists but breakfast entrepreneurs. On one side of the Atlantic, the Kelloggs were selling a range of scientific-sounding meat substitutes: Protose, Nuttose and Granose. On the other, in late Victorian and Edwardian England, people saw a boom in commercial vegetarian restaurants, the most popular of which was owned by tennis celebrity Eustace Miles. An Olympic silver medallist and expensively educated man with a muscular attitude to life, the so-called 'Nut King' established a shop-cum-school-cum-restaurant-cum-advice bureau that served over 1,500 meals per day and hosted lectures on lifestyle. The Eustace Miles Restaurant was more than just a place to eat vegetarian food. A centre of what was called *hygienic reform*, it was also a rehearsal ground for the masculine values of empire. All you needed to do to ascend the social hill, the establishment promised, was follow the man in cycling shorts and buy his patented 'Plasmon' biscuits.

Though Miles was a great beneficiary of vegetarian products, he made some outstanding efforts to distance himself from the label. Of the handful of books he published, the most vegetarian in focus is titled *Failures of Vegetarianism* (1902). The failure Miles refers to is not a nutritional failure, and nor is it an ideological one. The failure, for Miles, is one of branding – of making people, potential customers, feel bad. Miles saw with a businessman's clarity that the movement, up to this point, had painted the meatless diet as a matter of strict self-deprivation. Implicitly, this kind of valorisation of restraint served to shame the majority of people, self-conscious about their gluttonous desires. Miles's style of communication was free of austerity, shame and blame. Instead, he attempted to tempt his readers to join him. 'Experiment', he urged them, with the 'Simpler Foods', and let yourself judge the results. Dismissing 'the dogmatism of most "Vegetarians"' – an identity he tossed into air quotes – Miles invited his clients to imagine they were interested in Plasmon of their own free choice.

Perhaps they were, but the freedom to restrain oneself is a particular kind of pleasure – not quite the unbridled pleasure in food itself you might take in a simpler world. Miles was not proposing a simpler world, one in which people might eat happily together; his diet was to be practised in private, where you could hide your delight in abstemious self-improvement. The method was to 'live as strictly as you like while you are by yourself, so long as you do not lose your power to live to a certain extent as other people do when you are among them'. Miles himself was as thrilled with his own virtue as any AVS man, disdaining the 'impure-blooded' souls who found their pleasure in the 'Flesh foods', along with opium and tobacco. Every one of these substances struck Miles as 'unclean', as did eating more than one or two meals in a day. 'Many people do best without breakfast,' he suggests (he prefers to do without lunch). Not to worry if you find this difficult: 'A biscuit can be taken at midday.'

Whether movement vegetarians have organised their cause around slave abolition or imperialism, feminism or patriarchy, religion or state morality, the notion of virtue in abstention has repeatedly shown its hand, its bony, vague banality licensing a smorgasbord of horrors. 'You should wish to be healthy,' writes Miles, 'not from a selfish motive only, but because you must and will radiate health, and so help others in a practical way.'

The contemporary vegan alt-right, I am told, believe themselves to be helping 'make the world a better place' when they enact 'retaliatory violence' upon meat-eating degenerates. Their hallucinatory linkage of blood with soil – of whiteness with care for nature – grounds a morality of vegan purity that quotes from Hitler himself. Hindu nationalists also claim for themselves a world-improving ethic when they beat to death working-class, cow-eating Muslims.

When vegan liberals today claim to be making the world a better place, it is most often through an appeal to 'green living' – a tenuous faith in revolution one abstention at a time. This is not to say that diet should have no place in fomenting systematic change. As pioneers of the 1960s and 70s Alternative Food Movement saw, there can be political inspiration in having to find new pleasures. In her 1971 bestseller *Diet for a Small Planet*, researcher Francis Moore Lappé interspersed recipes with political analysis, teaching readers not just that the industrial-capitalist food system was responsible for world hunger, but also that a democratically run, plant-centred food system could yield delightful results. The bridge between personal inspiration and systemic change, however, is of course collective action. This is a fact that rarely surfaces in the movement discourses springing from Alternative Food. To be a proponent of farm-to-table, organic or plant-based eating, you need not be engaged in the struggle for a just economy – the kind of social arrangement that would make for a healthier planet or well-fed population at large. All you need is the cash to be able to model utopia for yourself.

Perhaps this is why today's environmentalists so often make the case for veganism in terms that reach no further than their own virtue. In 2018, *Guardian* columnist George Monbiot announced his 'conversion' to veganism as a straightforward means of 'reducing my impact on the living world'. His former love of cheese, he confessed, had been a matter of pure gluttony, but now he had the better of himself. 'We can withdraw our consent from this corruption,' he preached, and save both the planet and ourselves. Others have appealed not just to their own virtue, but moreover to their messianic duty to guide other people. For vegan influencer and bestselling author Ed Winters, the vegan who doesn't attempt to influence his neighbours is much like a person blessed with sight who simply looks on as a blind man walks into a hole.

By abandoning political economy – the effort to understand our rapacious world order in more systematic terms – many vegetarians have struggled to account for why their diet hasn't led to revolution, whether green, anti-capitalist or white supremacist. These are diets built on the woolliest sense of *doing the right thing*, a substitution of packaged political feeling for serious political commitment. A canvas, in other words, for all manner of ideologies other than those of human or animal social justice.

Without an understanding of how consumer choice is constrained by social class, and in turn how social class is shaped by relations of production, we do not see that it is not within everyone's power simply to change their diets. Until we devise an alternative economic system, cheap meat and cheap labour – both forms of cheap life – will be what keeps the food system profitable and food, for the majority, affordable. It is comforting to imagine that the world might transform through a sum of individual virtues. But virtue, in the end, is just a sentiment, dietary abstinence alone a mere pastime.

Why was it then that my own vegan diet *simply was* such a source of relief? Despite, that is, my scepticism of dietary choice as a thing to feel particularly good about? I found no sense of virtue or achievement in my choice to eat that way, yet I did feel a sense of refuge. Was this not, then, just another elaborate form of self-indulgence?

In the months that followed the start of my search for a relief meal, I began to explore this question in earnest. Was my veganism simply a distraction from meaningful political engagement? A prim preoccupation, looking for interesting types of gourd and making up for lost B12 with the bourgeois shibboleth of nutritional yeast? It seemed an important thing to ask, for example, when I watched a polite vegan on holiday slather margarine into the guts of an all-butter croissant. As though you could atone for all the butter in this world with brushstrokes of vegetable fat. It seemed important for me to ask one vaguely anorexic Thursday as I extracted hardened splodges of cheese from the surface of a mis-ordered pizza.

You might think that a person half-sane, anorexic or not, ought to doubt their own purposes here. Ought to ask what it achieves to move a disc of cheese to the side of a greasy plate instead of just moving it into your mouth where at least it will taste of something. There is something overtly strange, suspicious even, in attempts to call this kind of thing 'political'. The cow, you understand, has already been milked, the milk has already been cheesed. The cheese has already been purchased, slapped atop your pizza and pur-chased again by you. However surgically precise your cheese extraction, however clean your mouth, this episode will have done nothing to address The Bigger Picture. By which I mean the social and economic forces – the ones that lead to just about everything – that bring us to a situation where humans the world over live off animals and their juice.

But however you rationalised it, the splodge of cheese and all it stood for were things I simply couldn't stomach.

In fact, the only thing less appealing than patting myself on the back for being able to swear off cheese was the idea of patting myself on the back for being cynical enough to eat it. As though the only sane response to a fucked-up situation was to enjoy it as much as you could. To revel in the flavour of animal slaughter and animal exploitation and the human exploitation involved in both. My hesitance to fill my nose with the smell could not have been immediately useful, but better, I felt, to stand completely still than sprint in the wrong direction.

If anorexia didn't tend to have such a rapid downward momentum – pulling its sufferers ever deeper towards the ultimate giving up – I would say that the experience of having it is a bit like standing still. A bit like smelling poison in the water and not quite knowing what to do: you'll die if you drink it; you'll also die if you don't. You wait for further notice, make no decisions at all. You do not swallow, but you don't exactly *choose* not to.

I would not say I ever *chose* to be vegan. It felt to me more like something that happened. A bit like falling in love, which is in fact precisely where the fall into veganism started. I may have looked at Matt that New Year's Day like his diet was about to ruin our lives, but as my personal stash of milk got quite hard to finish alone, it began to feel a little unnecessary. And soon after that, as I started to get used to liquified oats, a little too much like milk. The reality of meat, i.e. animal flesh, came horribly into focus. The stuff that had been meant for the baby cow no longer felt cool in my throat.

Remembering this, I wondered if there might be other, bigger, ways to be inspired by what you ate. Falling in love had been enough to inspire a change of diet. But could a diet, in turn, be charged with other kinds of inspiration? A vegan diet had proven a useful way of persuading myself to swallow *just enough*, but if I wanted a life of abundance, perhaps this would take a vegan *worldview*. Perhaps I needed the example of vegans who'd prioritised more than food; more than their own supposed dietary goodness. People who'd done more than just recognise meat for what it was, and gone so far as to imagine alternative ways that humans might live – how they might reorganise their nourishment, their labour and their lives at the level of an entire society.

Perhaps the most promising figures were never going to be the vegan entrepreneurs: the ones who set out to sell a life-style, rather than considering the value of life. Eustace Miles may have made the biggest profit from his restaurant, but many other kinds of people had eaten there.

There had been, for example, the less well-known but also upper-class Constance Lytton, a woman who in 1908 had been radicalised when she saw a man beat up a sheep. Most of her social class might have thought this pretty normal, but Constance was significantly disturbed.

Constance was already vegetarian, but not for political reasons. Her aunt, a loyal disciple of dietary health reformers like Miles, had suggested a meat-free diet as a cure for her 'constitutional rheumatism'. Apparently, it worked, and Constance began to get used to life without meat. It was only then that a new concern for animal life began to *happen* in her mind. 'I realised, too,' she wrote, 'that all these years I had caused untold suffering that I might be fed.' She decided that her 'bill of fare' should no longer depend on any animal's premature death.

It is one thing, however, to care about untold suffering, another to do anything about it. It was only in 1908 that Constance's feeling for animal life became a politicised matter. Lytton was on holiday in Littlehampton with the Espérance Club – a dressmaker's cooperative she'd stumbled upon when looking for places to throw some inherited money. She found in the cooperative's women a 'spontaneous joy most refreshing'. She saw the women dance, singing folk songs, and felt the door open into a new paradise – a place where working women organised energetically for each other's rights. As Lytton developed a taste for working-class feminist politics, she began to witness other kinds of violence through this lens. Like the beating of a sheep, for example, which seemed to have broken free on the way to being slaughtered.

As Lytton recalls, a circle of jeering bystanders had penned the creature in place so it could be set back on its way to death. As she watched one of these 'gaolers' deal it a 'great cuff in the face', she felt an immediate insight into the basic workings of power. This man had such resentment for the sheep, which seemed to think it existed for more than human pleasure. Just like women, Lytton thought, who were expected to exist for nothing but the interests of men. 'How often', as she put it, 'women are held in contempt as beings outside the pale of human dignity, excluded or confined, laughed at and insulted because of conditions for which they themselves are not responsible.'

Lytton's career as a vegetarian may have begun with the relatively minor concerns of a sickly child, yet it raised in her a political consciousness that interlinked human and animal justice. After the sheep- and cooperative-inspired awakening, Lytton went to as many suffragist meetings as she could. Her new ambition was to immerse herself in the cause of women's rights. And the gatherings which, for Lytton, best exemplified 'the spirit behind this movement' were the breakfasts held for released political prisoners. Typically held at the Eustace Miles restaurant, these breakfasts were expressly meat-free. 'It is a strange fact', wrote the activist Maud Joachim in her 1908 memoir *My Life in Holloway Gaol*, 'that the ranks of militant suffragettes are mostly recruited from mild vegetarians.' Knowing what we know about Lytton's vegetarian journey, it doesn't seem all that strange.

It is true that the tone of vegetarian discourse in Edwardian Britain was generally far from militant, the Eustace Miles brand being all about befriending one's body, self-care and muscular strength. In other circles, however, the refusal of meat had little to do with the body. The French former Communard Élisée Reclus had written in 1901 that 'for the great majority of vegetarians, the question is not whether their biceps and triceps are more solid than those of the flesh-eaters', but rather 'the recognition of the bond of affection and goodwill that links man to the so-called lower animals'. For members of the Paris Commune, the idea was to preserve the horse and the cow, the rabbit and the cat 'either as respected fellow-workers, or simply as companions in the joy of life'. What could be more worthy of militancy?

It was this, more solidaristic, spirit that infused the diet of the suffragettes. Suffragette leader Charlotte Despard, for example, evokes in her writing 'the awakened instinct which feels the call of the sub-human, which says: "I am the voice-less. Through me the dumb shall speak."'

For Lytton, as for Despard, what struck someone dumb was not their animal inferiority, but the hard hand of power across their face. Specifically, Lytton was interested in how the 'monster of industrial capitalism' intensified oppressive dynamics between men and women, owners and workers, humans and animals. Society, she saw, had sacrificed the interests of both human and animal workers – human and animal meat – to the general pursuit of profit. Her dream was for industry one day to be 'bridled' so that it, instead, was the 'servant of humanity' – no longer a ruthless boss, it would become a 'fellow worker in the day-to-day glory of creation'. How better to make this happen, she and her sisters reasoned, than to start by giving women some demo-cratic power.

Unlike the health-conscious food reformers around her, the Temperance Vegetarians of the past and the wellness influencers of the future, Lytton was much less interested in *being* vegetarian than in acting in ways that championed those whom society treated as meat. Her admiration for the Espérance women was only enhanced by their disinterest in personal branding. 'How amazingly they played the game of incessantly advertising the cause without ever developing the curse of self-advertisement,' she observed. Words and principles, like diets, were one thing for Lytton; the strategies they inspired were another. There were plenty of words, for instance, flying around the Houses of Parliament. The Liberal government established in 1906 was full of men who called themselves Suffragist. Most of them stood in the way of any actual procedure that might move the country towards women's suffrage.

Lytton did not believe in virtue as an end in itself; she believed in political achievement. If an action, however virtuous, proved inadequate to bringing about change, her impulse was to escalate tactics until they broke through. While the National Union of Women's Suffrage Society contented itself with processions and petitions, Lytton, seeing very little movement from these, joined the Women's Social and Political Union. The WSPU believed the situation called for window smashing. When repeated civil disobedience was met with mass-jailing of its members, they continued to protest via a series of hunger strikes.

Government, WSPU members recognised, would rather not have women make a show of dying in their prisons. The strikes were therefore intended to put pressure on those in power either to release the hungry protestors or (ideally) give women the vote. Higher-class women were generally released before their bones began to show. For Lytton, no sooner had she dipped in a toe by refusing dietary 'extras' – Maltine, bananas and pudding – than she found herself released into the open air. Most hunger strikers, however, were subjected to grisly routines of force-feeding. Though perhaps less *publicly* offensive than letting women die, these feedings all but exemplified the women's brute reduction to meat. Lytton wanted to make the public understand this by whatever means she could. The plan she made was to disguise herself as so much meat to be fattened.

In other words, she planned to disguise herself as a working-class woman, and to get herself imprisoned again. She wheeled around the city of Manchester looking for ways to dress herself down – in her own words, to 'put ugliness to the test'. She got herself a cheap, cack-handed haircut and picked up a selection of poor woman's clothes. Lytton hid her expensive-looking face behind a thick pince-nez, which apparently worked so well that when her alias 'Jane Warton' went back out on the stone-throwing rampage, she was arrested without delay. In jail, at the first signs of hunger strike, Warton, unlike Lytton, was fed through a stinking tube.

In her life as an upper-class prisoner, Lytton's experiences of carceral cuisine did not strike her as the worst in the world. Her account of Holloway prison in her 1914 book *Prison and Prisoners* includes a description of some less-than-attractive meat, presented to her at the bottom of a dirty-looking tin. The loaves of bread, though, were appetising, and Lytton was free to save some for the end of the day if she thought she'd get more out of it then. She successfully asked a doctor for flannel underclothes and vegetarian food, explaining that a meatless diet had once cured her of a serious medical condition. Though prison authorities didn't know much about vegetarian food – Victoria Lidiard describes being given almost half a pound of butterbeans in Holloway in 1912 – they nevertheless made some effort to meet the upper classes' dietary requirements. Jane Warton had a little more trouble explaining the vegetarian thing. When the prison authorities tried to mainline Bovril down her neck, Warton begged for fruit juice instead. No such luck: the only choice she was granted was whether her jaws would be prized apart with the wooden or steel gag.

When Warton was first force-fed, Lytton tells us, the doctor explained to her that the steel gag would hurt and the wooden one would not. He told her not to force him to use the steel. When the dissident refused to open her mouth, he plied her teeth with the metal and, digging it into her gums until her mouth flew open with pain, he turned it 'much more than necessary' until her jaws gaped wide. Then came the tube, a monster of unwarranted girth and length, which choked the recipient on contact. The food was poured in, Lytton tells us, with a velocity that made her sick, and threw her limbs into convulsions. This prompted the doctors to lean on her knees while the wardresses pressed back her head. Once she had thrown up over all of them, the tube came out and she felt a mighty slap on the cheek. 'At first it seemed such an utterly contemptible thing to have done that I could only laugh in my mind,' she writes. 'Then I saw Jane Warton lying before me, and it seemed as if I were outside of her.' Warton, Lytton realised, was thoroughly despised and powerless to make the world care.

It is this, and not the actual difference in whether a woman drinks Bovril or fruit juice, that makes such an insult of the guard's indifference to Warton's vegetarian principles. It is the basic disallowance of these principles specifically for working-class women that demonstrates, via Lytton's testimony, the link between the violence that is done to non-human animals and the use of force against certain humans. 'Prisoners', Lytton writes, meaning prisoners like Warton, 'are made to feel in the presence of nearly every prison official that they are the scum of the earth, suspected of deceit, prejudged and found wanting; this has a paralysing effect on the prisoner's powers of expression.'

★

Proponents of the Maudsley model for treating anorexia point to evidence that patients have 'difficulties expressing emotion'. Patients, they observe, often present as 'blank-faced, reserved and stoical', 'enigmatic and bland'. I wonder to what extent this would still be the case were they not treated as scum of the earth. Were they not constantly suspected of deceit, prejudged and found wanting. Were they not stripped of the right to let their political commitments, or any values at all, shape the ways they eat, the ways they live.

There is a certain enlightened concern among professionals in the Royal College of Psychiatry that there are currently no vegan substances with which to tube-feed anorexic patients. It would have been nice if Lytton's prison guards had had such sympathy when her alter ego was asking for fruit juice. It would have been nice, but looked at another way, completely beside the point. If there are vegans who choose this diet because they genuinely cannot stomach the violence that goes into meat-making, how likely is it that they'll be grateful to have a vegan option forced through their nostrils – to be allowed to be vegan while they're pinned to a bed and reduced to anorexic meat? An anorexic who on any level wants to be free of their condition isn't looking to be forcibly fed – neither with well-meaning threats nor through a nasogastric tube. Instead, they are probably looking for reasons to want to live. If the goal is gradually to inculcate an appetite for life, it's difficult to imagine how a 'borderline substance' pumped through a medical hose is ever going to whet that hunger.

Among the anorexic population, there will certainly be vegans who couldn't give a shit about animal justice, nor about gender, class, racial or disability politics, or any of these interlocking causes. Yet to the extent that there are some who value this diet because they value the idea of a less exploitative world, should we not rejoice that, for all their inertia, they have any values at all? Is this not a welcome glimpse of some vision for the world – for the birds, mammals and fish that move around it? It seems unlikely that this vision will involve lifelong help with funnelling vegan food into their gut.

Perhaps such people would like to be able to eat not from fear of hospital treatment, but from assurance that eating will help them engage in the world. That it will help them to become a person – more than just a patient. A person with some purchase on the social world around them.

All of which suggests a vital need to rethink the way we discuss 'restriction'. No doubt, it is a problem that people starve to death because eating fills them with terror. Restriction of this nature represents nothing but the self-medication of unfreedom with unfreedom. And yet, this is not to say that restriction is always a fascist intervention, curtailing our freedom of choice or our sovereignty over our bodies. For Constance Lytton, a temporary hunger strike was a means of twisting power in favour of dispossessed women – of *starving so that others be better fed* with democratic agency. The strike may have been a suspension of participation in life, but only so as to expose the brutality people will foist in each other's mouths. It was, in certain ways, the ultimate withdrawal from the game of society, but only to make space for a future that might be more socially just.

Vegetarianism, for Lytton, was similarly a restraint that made space for political action; that quietly revolutionised a person's taste for more solidaristic ways of existing. To refuse to eat meat was not to purify the soul, nor even to preserve the lives of individual animals. Rather, it was a daily inspiration to care – to hold oneself accountable for how humans relate to each other and to animal life. This question of how they *should* relate to one another was not just a question for individuals at the table, but one for the entire social order. For Lytton, industrial capitalism functioned as a tool for reducing the meaning of life. A person's life, in the world she had inherited, was a unit of profitability – a thing to be sold for meat, or put to work, or made to sexually service male workers, bosses, owners. Her ambition, and that of her sisters, was to make the first steps towards a social world that valued living otherwise.

What does it mean that we so readily accept the logic of contemporary eating disorder treatments, which view restrictions of any kind, including the refusal of meat, as forms of non-cooperation? Perhaps we ought to ask what it is we are supposed to be cooperating in. If the aim is a healthier life, perhaps we ought to ask if there is more to life and health than calorie intake, female fertility, a number on a scale, a person's fitness to work. What if life were better measured by feeling alive, connected with the world, or faithful in the future possibility of justice? These are compelling motivations to nourish oneself, but they are not the things we typically think about when setting 'treatment goals', nor indeed the things we tend to think about when feeding ourselves in general.

When we try to train, cajole or force each other into eating 'correctly' in the name of our own good health, is this liberalism, granting freedom? Or is it fascism, stamping it down? The history of dietary control brings into focus how the distinction has never been all that clear. When a prison authority asks a dissident woman not to 'force' him to subject her to the steel gag, he plays into the common-sense wisdom that the tyrant is always the one who disturbs the status quo. However violent that status quo might be to women, working people and animals – it is conveniently labelled The Peace. And whatever disturbs The Peace can be construed as a kind of excess. Dietary restriction might sound like taking too little of something, but here, it is taking too little too much.

Since the English turn to Protestantism, and the rise of a governmental logic ordering modern society, a discourse of moderation, somewhat strangely, has sat at the heart of immensely powerful states. In England specifically, there have been very few transgressions we haven't been able to describe as *too much*. As historian Ethan H. Shagan points out in his book on *The Rule of Moderation* (2011), early modern Protes-tants saw cowardice not as insufficient courage, but rather too much self-love. Celibacy, vegetarianism and other strict abstentions from the flesh have been framed not as insuf-ficient desire but too much pride. *An-orexis* (literally 'not enough desire', or perhaps 'a desire not to') is by definition a kind of restraint – a drawing back from the world. And yet, we persist in interpreting this as a fascist excess of control.

'It takes violence to produce moderation,' writes Shagan, referring to the kinds of state, medical and capitalist coercion it takes to get us to behave in accordance with The Peace. Moderation, when it comes to the dietary ideal, is often the opposite of restriction – it is instead whatever constitutes obedience. It is a willingness to eat the right things, and in just the right amount, and look happy while you are doing it. Though the last hundred years have seen liberal societies organise diet in myriad rigid and uncompromising ways, always this organisation comes wrapped in a language of pleasure, democracy and choice.

When, for example, European fascists were insisting on purity diets, or making *cucina povera* into a matter of national pride, the Allied forces who fought them in the Second World War had their own prescriptive and patriotic food programmes. With nutritional science now a fixture of the technocratic playbook, wartime food programmes called on the power of diet to inculcate responsible citizenship. The US Food Fights for Freedom campaign asked citizens to compare their dietary intake to a set of Recommended Daily Allowances. It distributed scorecards and checklists so that people could log their eating habits in a 'Personal Nutritional Record', encouraging them to improve their scores and therefore the strength of the nation. Participants were encouraged to sign pledges to 'establish good food habits and follow them, knowing that by building a healthy body and strong nerves I can get more out of life myself and do more for others'. 'I'll be proud, too,' participants affirmed, 'of being a strong American.'

If all of this sounds dangerously close to fascist methods of social control, the US Committee on Food Habits was worried about that too. A 1945 report expressed concern that these kinds of approaches risked a level of 'authoritarianism in education and political practice' that would compromise the country's reputation as a land of the free. Yet rather than ceasing to govern through the control of dietary norms, the authorities simply resolved to find ways to make their programmes *feel* more democratic. The Committee discussed how best to pursue their social agenda while giving participants the experience of freedom. What they came up with, and what historian Charlotte Biltekoff has identified as the dominant system of authority in the twentieth-century US, was 'democratic social engineering'. Social engineering, as ever, but with a democratic vibe.

According to Biltekoff's history of food and health politics at this time, one of the landmark studies that made the case for democratic social engineering was carried out by psychologist Kurt Lewin, a member of the Committee on Food Habits. Lewin's study compared the power of two different teaching methods by testing them out on two groups of housewives. The aim was to get the housewives to absorb a set of ideas about how best to feed their families. The first cohort was simply lectured, the second engaged in a group discussion where the women were gently guided towards the same, predetermined conclusions. Participants, it turned out, were more suggestible when they felt like they were thinking for themselves. These faux discussions became the template for all future governmental efforts at food education.

They also form the backbone of many eating disorder treatments, which typically involve some kind of educational intervention. In the literature, these are defined as transmissions of information to patients in a way that might 'allow them to make correct health decisions'. In MANTRA, I was guided towards all kinds of rote conclusions about myself. Though each group discussion began with questions – *Am I overly focused on detail at the expense of the bigger picture? Am I finding it hard to be flexible and switch between different perspectives?* – it always somehow seemed to be the therapists who confirmed the final answers. Were we asked or were we told about which were our most helpful and unhelpful interactions with others? About the effects of starvation on our bodies, about a day in the lives of our stomachs? Through a series of 'behavioural experiments' with only one conclusion, we learnt from total strangers about the impact of our 'thinking styles' on our intimate lives, about our identities, our 'best possible selves', our qualities, values and struggles. An overview of the method explains that 'the therapist constantly has to maintain the momentum for moving the patient in the direction of change, that is, in the direction of healthy eating and weight gain'.

These may have been reasonable things for the therapists to want, but they weren't how I defined change. Studies of educational interventions, in true technocratic form, ask no questions about how patients might define a good 'health outcome'. They emphasise how education 'reduces the use of healthcare' in its aftermath, thus 'minimising the general burden of the condition'. Their interest is more in the needs of healthcare systems than the tricky subjectivities of their patients. It remains unexplored whether these treatments reduce the use of healthcare because patients are satisfied, or simply because they recognise that food education was never what they needed. 'Healthy eating and weight gain', without change of a more meaningful kind, are liable simply to keep patients afloat in lives they do not want.

Relief can be as visceral a signal as any of what a person wants – how they experience change for the better. Relief can be as simple as a pizza that tastes of tomatoes rather than guilt – of deep, salty dough and dusty dried oregano. Clearly, there existed some part of me that cared for something other than cruelty, that wanted to show this to my stomach. That wanted my mouth to taste of something other than indifference to the lives of others.

The more I nursed this thought over ethically ambiguous encounters with dairy, the less plausible fascism seemed as the link between my vegan and anorexic tendencies. Neither, in truth, had very much to do with self-punishment or purification. What they did have in common was their status as forms of non-participation – one in the violence of meat-making, the other in the violence of everything.

Yet while my veganism might therefore have looked like a branch of anorexic withdrawal, non-participation and total retreat are not the same thing. Anorexia is a suspension of action that leaves little room for making new plans. It is a species of withdrawal that folds in on itself and chokes the imagination. Veganism, by contrast, is a suspension of 'normal' eating, but one that is founded on a vision of new ways to eat and to live. As a diet alone, it is not a meaningful end in itself, but it is a welcome inspiration, as people like Lytton have shown, for more strategic kinds of political action. Anorexia made me hungry; veganism gave me a way to eat. It gave me a way to eat pizza: with anything other than cheese.

Anorexia, while far from a hunger strike, or anything so active as protest, did bring to my attention a problem in my relation to the world. Its effect, however, was the opposite of stirring me to any real political response. Anorexia is a hairline crack in the surface of bureaucratic eating, but proposes nothing new in its place. If I was going to restrict my diet, I was going to need to bolster it too. I was going to have to get my ideas from more than one floppy slice of Marinara.

3

You Gorge

Bolstering my diet was easier said than done. I already had some experience of trying, and struggling, to do this on command. The summer before I even heard about the magic mushroom trial, before any search for 'empowerment', I had at least made some effort to gain a bit of weight – the more typical medical advice.

People often said they were jealous of my weight-gain assignment and at times I was jealous of myself. The doctors had advised that I become a certain size, and that I make this happen by eating. The size was quite a lot bigger – obviously – than the size at which I would start. Mathematically speaking, the goal was equivalent to what I would achieve were I to slice my body in four, double the mass of one of the pieces and roll them all back into one. Surely, I imagined, this would take a level of eating that couldn't help but be fun.

It seemed I had arrived on the threshold of an authorised satisfaction largely unknowable to mortals. What calibre of otherworldly edibles could be high enough for the occasion? Never had my stomach felt so open to treats – doughy and greasy and warm. I could bury entire hot loaves inside of myself and brush my teeth with buttercream icing. Breakfast on melted-down chocolate bars and dine on deep-fried pasta. And why not throw in a treat or two I didn't even like, simply because I could? I fantasised working through boxes of those supermarket desserts, feeling their workaday sweetness disappear down my neck and sinking from the world of self-awareness. I would surface, I imagined, in a state so sated as to sugar the rest of my life.

In a way, I thought, if the point of self-starvation hadn't been death, then it must have been something like this. All that hunger having pointed, in fact, towards the bliss that would eventually end it. Food may have been a kind of nightmare, but it was also, in a sense, my north star. Except that there was nothing, when the moment came to gorge, that lived up to that celestial status.

Nothing tasted as good to me as eating felt bad. Which is unsurprising, given my consent to gain weight had had little to do with suddenly wanting to eat. I had wanted some of the side-effects of eating – a good head of hair, the approval of my friends, a set of fully functional organs – yet while these things had compelled me to give it a go, what they couldn't do was make me do it gladly.

For Catherine of Siena – the one who drank the pus in Chapter One – no food was worthy of feasting on but Jesus himself. In this, she was much like any other 'holy anorexic', for whom nothing tasted as good as eucharistic flesh. Bread-as-body, wine-as-blood, like the sweetest buttercream icing God himself could confect. Like lamb 'roasted not boiled' on the 'spit of the cross', according to Saint Catherine. Her abstention from ordinary food was never meant to last forever – instead, it was simply

preparation for this ultimate eating event. All that starvation pointing to the bliss that would finally end it.
When Christ did eventually come to her, offering a suck
on the wound in his side, his promise, according to one
of the saint's hagiographies, was 'such delight that your
very body, which for my sake you have denied, shall be
inundated with its overflowing goodness'.

Only until that moment, Catherine reasoned, would she
have to take pleasure in pain – the pain of starvation, for
example, but also of drinking dirt. The filthier the preparation diet, the cleaner the relief meal would seem. And the
purer the encounter with Jesus would be, the sweeter it made
the pus. 'Never in my life', Catherine claimed, 'have I tasted
food or drink sweeter or more exquisite,' as she wiped her
mouth clean of the juice from a dying woman's putrefying boob.

Jesus, Catherine thought, had made his flesh into food
and 'there was no other means for man to be satisfied'. This
romance with the perfect food makes some sense of the
apparent contradiction between the holy anorexics' aversion
to food, and their evident obsession with it. Juliana of Cornillon, whose longing for the eucharist began in her teenage
years, along with her tendency to starve in preparation, also
spent her life attempting to institute the feast of Corpus
Christi, planned as a holy meal to end all hungers. When her
monastic superiors tried and failed to make her eat normal
food, it wasn't that she wanted nothing. She explained that
what she wanted was simply not of this earth: 'I want better
and more beautiful food.'

It seems it wasn't eating itself that gave these holy women
such problems, but rather the world that ordinary food

represented. It is easy to read this rejection in purely spiritual terms, as though the only thing they found debased in the mortal realm was that it wasn't heaven. Medieval historians have taken a more sociological approach. Rudolph Bell, for one, noted that the drive to self-starve was especially prominent among women who had been married. He theorised this revulsion at marriage as a revulsion at the request to hand one's body over to a man. Caroline Walker Bynum takes a more materialist view of marriage – not just as an individual property exchange, but an engine of social inequality. Reading the *vitae* or 'lives' of medieval saints, Walker Bynum detects a species of discomfort or guilt among the privileged stratum of girls from which the saints were drawn. Most, she observes, were educated and rich, and seemed anxious to renounce a life of inherited wealth while the people around them starved.

Medieval Europe was certainly a time of frequent famine – perhaps an awkward time for these girls to feel trapped on a path to securing their own advantage. Throughout the later thirteenth century, people were alert to the breadcrumbs of selfishness and greed. The air was thick with stories of merchants hoarding food as the poorest peasants killed their own children, or left them to die.

One such villain in Italy – a man who stashed away roasted crusts of bread and sacks of trodden-down meal – was found dead in his home in 1286. The townspeople who discovered him and his hoard of moulding crusts assumed he must have been taken by the devil. Children dragged his stiff, naked corpse through the street and tossed it off a bridge onto some gravel. If gluttony, then, was considered at this time an especially salty sin, it wasn't just for doctrinal reasons. We are talking, here, specifically of gluttony in the absence of a glut.

Was I looking for better or more beautiful food than the dumplings at Xi'an Famous Foods? A fortnight after agreeing to the weight-gain assignment I had gone to the USA to guest-teach a seminar series on art. After the job was over, I spent a few days in New York, determined to enjoy the opportunity and eat some big city grease. I didn't have shed-loads of money to spend, or any kind of appetite for steak, so the obvious way to achieve this as a tourist was to hang around fast-food chains.

There I was, then, tentatively chewing on vegetables swaddled in dough. The dumplings squatted in a pool of speckled oil that shone livid from a white paper plate. Each mouthful was reliably tasty, but also a reliable ordeal. Some-thing in the experience made me even more conscious than usual that I was, in fact, *eating*. Perhaps it was the vivid colour of the oil or the strangeness of the city. Perhaps it was my weight-gain mission. Spice and garlic hung in my throat like a record of every bite. None of it tasted as perfect as the guilt felt bad.

Perhaps there is something unbeautiful in a hyped-up res-taurant chain. The kind of internet noodle sensation where the whiter clientele, for all their performative enthusiasm for 'authentic' Chinese food, must be pleaded with by lami-nated signage not to fear the abundance of oil. Carrying the dishes of hot sour sustenance over to our bench, Matt, my travel companion, asked if I had seen the till-side informa-tion on how 'Chili oil is your friend'. This oil, infused with over thirty different spices, was, according to the sign, not as 'scary' as I thought. I recognised my uptight, Western self as the audience for this sign, and felt the proportionate shame.

It is true that the so-called Western psyche has been known to run in fear of liquid fat. We are wary, perhaps, of what enjoying such things might reveal to us of ourselves. Our greed, let's say, for entitlement to an oil-slicked existence, frictionless at others' expense. 'We might be hogging the Earth's resources', writes Barbara Ehrenreich of this group, 'and tormenting the global working class, but at least we're not indulging the ancient human craving for fat.' Everyone, in other words, 'wants to be rich, but no one wants to be known as a "fat cat"'.

We know there is a special hot place in the inferno for the greedy white bourgeoisie – hungry for more than their share of this mean little world. It starts, we believe, in childhood, by which point these people have already gone bad with unjust privilege. Like those brats whose financial capacity to buy up Wonka bars wins them all a poisoned ticket to chocolate hell. There in that illusion of Eden, we watch their bodies, bloated with gluttony, get stuffed into industrial pipes. Or blown into human beachballs of big, blue gastric distension. The reading and movie-watching public takes this kind of thing in their stride, absorbed in cheerfully rooting for that skinny little urchin Charlie.

I was a person who had taken my education in the wages of greed to university level, filling myself with the literature and history of decadent Rome. One of the first Latin texts my cohort of Classics undergraduates enjoyed was Petronius's first-century satire of nouveau-riche excess. In 'Trimalchio's Dinner', an episode in the author's *Satyricon*, the titular character, all money and supposedly no sense, embarks on a gross display of edible wealth. In a sequence as deliciously jarring as an incompetent brass band, food is served amidst the blaring of an entire orchestral assembly. Trimalchio thinks there should be *culture* at the table, by which he means acrobats, food-based astrology, dog-based hunting re-enactments. Best of all, he treats his diners to a reading of the records of his estate, detailing assets he didn't even know he had.

Like Trimalchio himself, the household chef leans naively into an overabundance of choice, prioritising the theatrics of the culinary gimmick over the diners' actual pleasure. He is skilled in modelling fish from the bellies of pigs, and pigeons from bacon, doves from ham and chickens from pork knuckles. In comes a circular tray, around which are displayed some edible counterparts for each of the zodiac signs – the womb of an 'unfarrowed' sow for Virgo, a piece of beef for Taurus. When the guests become depressed at the sight of this fare, the host only makes things worse, informing them that dinner is still to come; that this is all merely the sauce.

Trimalchio's gluttony is punished, in the story, with his guests' extravagant disdain. To study the tale is to punish his archetype with laughter. My classmates and I found the episode's final scene particularly funny, our cruelty having matured, perhaps, more quickly than our intellects. Here, Trimalchio achieves his greatest failure to read the room and makes a play to be pre-emptively eulogised. Calling for wine to be poured into a punch bowl, he slurs at his guests to imagine they are mourners at his funeral feast. He stretches out on the couch to a makeshift dirge. 'Pretend I'm dead,' he whines, 'and say something nice about me.'

Poor Trimalchio simply adores being rich. He says he hopes he will enjoy food and wine when he is dead just as much as he loves it in life. Yet with that final, desperate plea for approval, we suspect he fears that perhaps he might not. Roman religion was not entirely sympathetic to lifestyles like his. Though Roman manners may have been profligate compared with the Christian morality that displaced them, they were not without their codes of restraint. Semi-historical texts are as brutally frank about this as excoriating satires.

None more brutal, perhaps, than accounts of the third-century emperor Elagabalus. As childlike as Trimalchio in his gluttonous excess, the Elagabalus who appears in ancient records was, by some people's measures, literally a child. Having ascended to the throne at fourteen, he apparently displayed such glee in opulence that even the Romans saw fit to interpret his behaviour as evil. The meals he laid on, it is said, involved such items as cockscombs snatched from the heads of living birds, camels' heels and nightingales' tongues. If his palace attendants were lucky, they could look forward to heaving platters of flamingos' brains, parrots' heads and peacocks. Banquets might involve twenty-two courses and sex with a woman between each one. Equally, guests might be served what seemed to resemble the emperor's food, only sculpted out of ivory, wax or wood. Rather than gorging and fucking between each course, they'd simply drink and wash their hands, pretending as though they had eaten.

Elagabalus, they say, also liked to drink himself silly after dinner. He drank so much that people mused it was as though he were drinking from one of his swimming pools – pools he refused to swim in unless they were perfumed with saffron or similar. A needy young man with more at his disposal than a man could possibly need, he carved out around him a zone of capricious, dangerous want. A menu might be composed (why not?) of just one substance – ostrich for every course. Or all one colour – everything blue – or mixed with semi-precious stones. His guests' sense of awe was more important to him than not only their nutrition, but even their survival. Hence the tale of his subjecting one party to a fatal avalanche of flowers. Petals, thundering down from a makeshift ceiling, are reported to have smothered some diners to death.

By the logic of the emperor's biographers, this kind of deranged behaviour posed a threat to the Roman city's sacred pact with the Gods. Peace in Rome, it was generally believed, was contingent on its citizens' good behaviour. To disturb such a peace could expose the whole city to unspeakable divine retribution, which perhaps explains the private retribution exacted on the emperor. After four years of rule, Elagabalus and his mother were stabbed to death by his soldiers, after which his body was stripped and trawled, gaping, through the dirty streets of Rome. No such monster was going to be given a proper Roman burial. Instead, he was loaded with weights and thrown into the river. No safe passage for him into any kind of palatable afterlife.

Even, then, before Christian rule brought in stricter norms of moderation, gluttons have had to fear the harshest punishment. Fill yourself with fat, we believe, and you are likely to disgorge all kinds of harm over others – harms that will come back to engulf you in this life or the next. Elagabalus's soul, having left his roughed-up corpse, could expect to endure an eternity just as bleak as the medieval breadcrust hoarder. In the thousand years between them, little seems to change in the moral economy of eaters and eaten – that merciless morality captured in the paintings of Hieronymus Bosch.

Bosch's *The Last Judgement*, dated to 1482, remains a hell-scape for our times. In a fantasia of sin and punishment, we find gluttons meeting their ends as sentient kitchen ingredients. Just about discernible, a soup of veteran overeaters churns in a dimly rendered cauldron. In the foreground, a wimple-clad, reptilian cook is heating a face in a frying pan. Tossing it together with a hand and a leg, she is poised to serve it with eggs. Behind her is the spit-speared body of a man – a rotisserie human in progress. Having faced their final judgement after a lifetime of supposedly thoughtless over-consumption, Bosch's gluttons are thoughtfully, carefully, deliberately, vengefully cooked. There is, in the Christian fear of having eaten too much, a certain appeal to justice – a certain appeal to the notion that punishing gluttons might be fair.

In life, we suppose there is justice in making sure we are eaten by guilt, engulfed by a psychic weather blown in from more God-fearing times. In Dante's inferno, an invention of fourteenth-century literature, the gluttons are subjected to the kind of physical discomfort many anorexics will know. Caught in a private micro-climate of bone-chilling hail and snow, they are destined to be cold forever. Punished for directing their lives at the selfish pursuit of bodily pleasure, they are recomposed of bodily distress. Perhaps, when we subject ourselves to this kind of chronic discomfort, we are simply trying to pre-empt what we believe is already our fate. Get it all over with now, or at least put in a decent rehearsal for the hell that is to come.

★

I had no such fear, as an undergraduate student of greed, that I myself might be condemned for my gluttony. I was nothing like an emperor, nor any other powerful man, overguzzling at a cost to the unfortunate 'eaten'. I was a woman, and women were authorised by Nigella Lawson to be shameless in eating what we liked. A staple of mine in those years was Nigella's Eggs in Purgatory – a kind of lava-based concoction. A thing to be gobbled after soaking your insides, as I liked to, with cranberry-sweetened vodka.

'After any evening of carousing,' writes Nigella, 'this dish of eggs cooked in a fiery tomato sauce can feel like heaven.' Purgatory, she explains, though the sauce may look like hell, is in fact a mere gateway to the good place. A holding pen for those who have died in grace but are not quite ready for paradise. I imagined, at the time, that if heaven was life on the other side of study, those vodka-spiked limbo-years of sensual awakening were, at least, a promising preview. Nigella likes to think of the dish as referring to Dante reaching purgatory at dawn – golden yolks rising, hopeful, out of a night in the crimson inferno.

'Yes I know,' writes Nigella. 'I wouldn't push it too far either, but you can't blame a person for trying.' The point was simply to be playful, dismissive with hell, and all who would condemn a woman to it. For Nigella, who is not herself a Catholic, there is no greater hell on earth than hunger, no greater reward for women's historical suffering than to treat yourself to an early oily afterlife of pleasure. Plunging crusty canoes of bake-at-home baguette into the river of yolky tomato, my housemate and I would practise being kind to our ravenous, womanly selves.

Nigella, that boom-box of appetite, preaches pride in earthly delights. Not just a quiet self-acceptance, but a noisy declaration of rights. Love of eating, according to her doctrine, may not be *teachable* as such, but, as charismatic leaders are prone to, she hopes to be able to *convey* it. 'I have nothing to declare but my greed,' says Nigella – a fact she plays out in her television shows each time she descends on a midnight fridge, its glow haloing her dive into whimsical bonus meals. Cold fish fingers, stuffed into bread and applied like an oxygen mask; a heap of ice cream, studded with nuggets of crumbling leftover cookie and mercilessly drowned in fudge sauce. Nigella doesn't just preach, but embodies, the idea that no one should regret their own indulgence. To women unsure of this sentiment, she counsels: 'You are entitled to eat.'

At thirty, it seemed my belief in such a straightforward thought had lacked endurance or strength. By the time of my weight-gain assignment, I had proven I no longer felt entitled to eat in the least. The freedom I had felt in discovering myself to be a woman deserving of 'more' had withered over time as I learnt to experience myself as a privileged cunt. As a student I'd been vaguely aware of checking my whiteness from time to time as well as my middle-class childhood. It took some time, however, to sense that these facts might make a difference to my status 'as a woman'. It was all very well, I thought, to reclaim the rights you've been denied, but what if there was nothing to reclaim? What if I was in fact a specific genre of woman who had *always* been entitled, by society, to eat.

It is only, if we're serious, particular types of greed that are truly despised in this world. Greeds perhaps less eloquent, less photogenic, than Nigella's. For although Nigella wants us to eat, she wants us to eat in a particular way. She wants us to practise the manners – the class – to savour what we scoff. She wants us to feel no guilt for what we put into our mouths, yet she wants us to be adequately grateful. Food is a privilege, she tells us – a fact to be mentally rehearsed in every moment of eating. 'When I eat chocolate,' she writes, 'I linger over every square, deciding which I will let melt slowly in my mouth, which I chomp on rapaciously, quickly, feeling how different the sensations are . . . [A]t no time do I want to carry on once the exquisite rapture has receded, and it becomes mindless or automatic.' She is 'extravagant', she insists, but 'never wasteful'.

In Nigella's self-presentation as a thoughtful lover of food, there are shades of Brillat-Savarin's distinction between the glutton and the *gourmand*. 'Gourmandism', he writes in *The Physiology of Taste*, 'combines the elegance of Athens, the luxury of Rome, and the delicacy of France.' It 'unites careful planning with skilled performance, gustatory zeal with discrimination; a precious quality which might well be called a virtue, and is at least the source of our purest pleasures'. From this Enlightenment perspective, gourmandisms like Nigella's 'deserve nothing but praise and encouragement'. It is 'by no means unbecoming in women; it suits the delicacy of their organs, and compensates to some degree for the pleasures they must forgo, and the ills to which Nature has seemed to condemn them'. As though in clairvoyant anticipation of the Domestic Goddess herself, Brillat-Savarin concludes that 'there is no more charming sight than a pretty gourmand in action'.

Perhaps this is why, in a classic episode of one of her shows – a tribute to dishes Nigella deems 'trashy' – our extremely un-trashy instructor radically skimps on a key ingredient of Elvis Presley's Fried Peanut Butter and Banana Sandwich. The original version is featured in the 1996 documentary *The Burger & the King*, in which the singer's culinary life is both remembered and recreated by those who cooked and ate with him. Elvis's cook Mary Jenkins demonstrates the proper way to make the special sandwich. After she has thickly spread two slices of toasted white bread with peanut butter, she lays a banana, sliced into coins, in the centre, and drops the sandwiched pieces into a skillet full of butter. Great dollops have already been melted, forming a sizzling bath for the bread. As it browns, she scrapes in several globs more so the frying is liquid and loud. 'He wanted 'em real rich,' explains Jenkins, who turns the slab gently, over and over and over. The point would seem to be to let the thing turn golden slowly so the butter seeps right to the centre. In total, the recipe calls for four ounces of the stuff, which Nigella slims down to just one. Nigella's version softly hits the base of a non-stick pan, merely slicked with a sensible pat. Rather than sizzling, it squeaks, standing tall, dry-crusted and dignified throughout the brief process. Jenkins's version breaks down into a unified splodge. It glistens from base to brow.

Nigella is heedful of the 'kamikaze' calorie count even in her slimmed-down version. 'I honour the King,' she admits, 'but I can't be him.' Indeed, it is hard to imagine her, satin-robed and serene, poking around the midnight fridge and extracting the 8,000-calorie peanut butter and jelly sandwich that was purportedly Elvis's favourite. Fool's Gold it was called at the Denver deli he made famous for a while. Each individual loaf-sized behemoth took in a pound of bacon and a jar of each variety of spread. 'Elvis's whole life was built on a lot of boredom,' explains a friend of the star. He remembers a day when the two of them flew to Denver for no reason other than to sample the sandwich. Without descending from the plane, they took delivery on the runway of twenty-two rounds of Fool's Gold. As soon as the King had eaten, they turned the plane around and flew straight home to Memphis.

Nigella describes her tribute to the fried Elvis sandwich as sustenance to 'restore the fragmenting self'. She has no interest in the unhappy search, as she puts it, for 'mind-numbing obliteration'. Yet in *The Burger & the King*, Elvis's friends unanimously summon the image of a man who sought to bury his aching heart in peanut butter, butter and bread. Born in the Great Depression in Tupelo, Mississippi to parents poorer than poor, Elvis was raised, essentially, to eat whatever didn't eat him. According to a childhood friend, who – though himself badly off at the time – considered the Presleys official 'white trash', Elvis never got over overindulging in the things he was denied as a squirrel-eating child.

Nigella can't eat like Elvis – why should she? – but nor could Elvis have eaten like her: secure enough to linger over mouthfuls, graceful and grateful for every crumb. Flirting, let's say, with 'trashy' but never actual trash. Nigella would make this distinction clear in an interview in 2022 when she was mined for advice on handling Christmas in a cost-of-living crisis. How to make the dinner go further, she was asked, with food costs and energy bills so high? Her response boiled down to a suggestion that the masses simply eat less. People should eat with more sophistication, she implied; people should eat like she did. Nigella cringed, for instance, at the ignorant folk who think that starters have any part in Christmas Day; at the trashier contingent inclined towards 'obscene overindulgence' for simply not knowing any better. 'You want to feel full and grateful,' she said, 'but you don't want to be a bloated wreck.' Gluttony might be fine if handled 'interestingly', but you wouldn't want to take it too far. Gourmandism, for Brillat-Savarin, is an 'impassioned, reasoned and habitual preference for everything which gratifies the organ of taste'. It is 'the enemy of excess'. By contrast, 'it is well known that savages eat to excess and drink themselves into a stupor whenever an opportunity presents itself'.

No stranger to a stupor, Elvis could not have been Nigella and nor, in fact, could a Trimalchio ever have learnt the culinary manners of Petronius, his author. Trimalchio, you see, is a former slave, Petronius a governor friend of Nero. Trimalchio's excesses are funny not because he is simply absurd but because he has no taste. For Trimalchio is not just rich, he is *nouveau riche*, his entertainments nouveau riche entertainments. His giddy loves and morbid fears are the loves and fears of a man who knows what it is like to have been shackled. His gimmicks are the style of a man who has failed to understand that more is not actually more. Not, in any case, by the rules of any respectably opulent Roman.

As for Elagabalus, he may have been an emperor but, cru-cially, he wasn't a Roman. At least not in the eyes of those whose 'historical' documents have survived. A child of Syrian heritage, Elagabalus betrayed his otherness in various cultural markers – circumcised penis, porkless diet – all of them recorded in tones of anti-Eastern suspicion. When ancient historians describe his greed, they are not conjur-ing the typical greed of a powerful Roman autocrat; this is a greed of alien effeminacy and excess. The emperor's cruelties, exotically evil, are charged in the texts with a mystical, ritual energy. They are not just obscene; they are suspicious.

In Rome, the avarice of Easterners was a well-worn stereotype. Especially suspect, in the popular imagination, was their zealous devotion to unfamiliar gods. Elagabalus had been named for his early priesthood of the god Elagabal of Emesa, whom he worshipped in the form of a conical black stone. As emperor, he gave this stone the highest rank in the Roman pantheon, as though you could simply make Jupiter the Best and Greatest . . . second best. Though the ancient histories aim their censure at the emperor's excess – his habit of mixing pearls into rice – this accusation of 'greed' may have been a mere proxy for less sayable bigotries and fears. More of a code, in other words, for the xenophobic sentiments common to ancient Roman readers.

Most contemporary historians doubt there can be much of substance or truth in the stories of Elagabalus's greed. Their function, no less than that of satire, may have had more to do with checking social hierarchy than documenting fact. The point was to plant a suspicion not just of those who wanted 'too much' but, more specifically, those whose wants were bigger than their status. Even an emperor, depending on the colour of his skin, can overstep the mark.

Sometimes it is hard to know what kind of greed you are indulging – justified or overentitled. Sometimes, it feels easier to safely undereat, or not to eat at all. Especially when no kind of gluttony feels particularly useful or fun. At the time of my weight-gain assignment, I felt no pull towards the kinds of routine binge Nigella dismisses, yet so was I also sceptical of her own, more self-congratulatory style of gorging. Wasn't the idea that 'eating is a privilege' something the privileged might want to be concerned about, rather than so profoundly grateful for? Our world, after all, isn't strictly lacking in food, which is widely overproduced, nor are we missing the technological means to distribute it better. The problem, when it comes to the widespread malnourishment of the poor, surely cannot be reduced to how much a person of privilege chooses to feed themselves.

Inequality, in other words, does not issue directly from whether the rich are careless or grateful. We find ourselves at the mercy of social arrangements – historically feudal, now capitalist – which ensure that certain people are better fed than others. Today, a feeding system grounded in profit has globally cheated the poor. In the Global South, it has diminished the bodies of those who labour over food they are forced to export elsewhere. In the North, where food so often overflows, it is still mostly only the rich who can afford to eat the kind of good, nourishing food it is worth writing essays about; to follow dinner with the kind of chocolate it would be nice to savour slowly in single, melting, squares; the kind of food it is actually possible to enjoy in splendid moderation.

At the earlier end of the so-called 'obesity epidemic', the cultural theorist Lauren Berlant noted in 2007 that for the first time in the history of the world, the overfed were no longer the wealthiest compared to the poor and the starving. 'Obesity' and starvation, wrote Berlant, were mirror symptoms, throughout the world, of the malnourishment of the poor. No longer could it make sense to imagine overeating as a privilege of unjust souls. The injustice was in morally censuring the fat for their psychic expressions of want.

Behind the fact of undernourishing overeating lie various social realities: long working days and cheap fast food, the nonexistence of leisure, the inaccessibility of pleasures less reliable or immediate in nature. There is also, however, the related urge to make things feel less bad. This is not to say make things better, which would imply that there are social solutions to be found in a giant peanut butter sandwich. We are talking simply, to quote Berlant, about a 'small vacation from the will' – a will so often exhausted from the pressure of *doing better*. We live in a world that rewards very few for their efforts to make a 'good life' – to perfect themselves enough to secure a decent job, a nice home, a willing partner in the project of upward mobility. Perhaps the average glutton wants a break from all this – from the pressure of treating their body as a temple of bourgeois achievement. Perhaps they want to pretend, as they gorge, as though they could remove their body from time. To eat to excess, thinks Berlant, could create a 'meaningful or meaningless feeling of well-being' – a shudder in the moment, a fair-enough fantasy of *like there's no tomorrow.*

Of course, if a situation like this one is ever to change, we need some sense of a meaningful tomorrow. 'Paradoxically,' writes Berlant, 'there is less of a future when one eats without an orientation towards it.' This must be as true of self-starving behaviour as it is of binging to death. If you are going to assist in bringing about change, you must be able to survive your own diet.

Just as it might be soothing to fill yourself up when life has systematically short-changed you, it can be soothing not to eat when you feel as though you have been oversupplied. Your mind feels smooth and motionless, even as the body goes on digesting, or trying, with no object to digest. Yet neither extreme of diet, however calming, can be credited with making things better. Each, to the contrary, seems to betray some variety of despair. Despair, in the Christian tradition, is a sin worse than gluttony itself. A sin so terrible, in fact, that the Church refuses to forgive it.

Unlike the 'mindless' glutton so pitied by Nigella, the subject of despair, in Catholic doctrine, involves their whole mind in their sin. To despair is to have experienced an intellectual change – to have *decided*, rather than merely intuited, that there is no possible hope of salvation. Despair is a sin that betrays a disbelief in humans' capacity to do better than we are doing, or – worse – in God's capacity to provide us with the strength. In secular discourse, despair would seem to signal a disbelief in the capacities of society at large. Society, we think, can never provide – the social order isn't going to change. It is desperate, to think of humanity as a mere collection of mouths, each one hungrily gathering pleasure to itself and caring for itself alone. Whether it be the pleasure in starvation, a binge or a lingered-over indulgence.

At least the holy anorexics had faith in a better and more beautiful life to come. I myself held out no such hope. There was no food that looked to me like Jesus, not even those slices of toast you saw on the internet that seemed to have popped out printed with a dark brown image of Christ. All logic aside, I wonder if some part of me needed an impossible assurance: that there'd always be enough to go round. Not content to meet this need with mere fantasies of heaven, I would have to make do with nothing.

So filled was I with this feeling and my powerlessness to resolve it that I'd struggle to sustain a conversation. At various stages of lifting, inspecting and relinquishing those dumplings, I had no idea what Matt, or I, was saying. Were we talking about something 'of the moment' like the change to abortion rights; the current ethics of masking and its grounding in ritual or science? The people around us or the people in the queue for the club the night before? Or some already over-discussed anxiety like rent or cultural labour? Some blah like why it seemed so impossible to buy a bulb of garlic in the city of New York? All of this was drowned in a broth of rumination, issuing from an over-theorised dumpling.

Despair was like a faithless decision of the mind, in other words, to go gently insane. To emerge, I would need a vision as seductive as the one I had once found in the theatre of Nigella. But Nigella's was a philosophy, a feminism, a dream that stood outside the world of circumstance and means; above the earthly domains of poverty, on the one hand, and class-conscious shame on the other. The fantasy had begun to feel like a seductive call to the impossible. The dicta, 'food is pleasure', 'food is essential', 'food is life', like bids to seduce a prisoner into believing they could simply walk free.

'[The] internal requirement toward excellence which we learn from the erotic must not be misconstrued as demanding the impossible from ourselves nor from others.' I had been teaching Audre Lorde in those classes for which I had flown to the USA, basing my seminars around an idea that seemed convincing enough in writing: that desire is politically pro-ductive and that art, which touches desire, must therefore have a chance at being politically productive too. In 'Uses of the Erotic', an essay from 1978, the self-described 'Black woman warrior poet' writes of the power in sensual experience.

A power, she warns, that cannot be harnessed until it has been collectively produced.

Productive desire, I suggested to the students, did not just mean wishful thinking: *I want therefore I can*. Instead, it had something to do with people wanting near each other, the threads of their various wants forming a supercharged tangle that could make something happen in the world.

'Do you think the students cared?' I asked, since Matt had been sitting in on the class.

He said he might go and get an extra plate of noodles, and maybe one of those cucumber salads.

'The sharing of joy, whether physical, emotional, psychic or intellectual,' writes Lorde, 'forms a bridge between the sharers.' Her idea is that in feeling joy together, people might find themselves better equipped to confront the awkward fact of the differences between them. Lorde, I assumed, was mostly talking about being a lesbian, and what lesbians did for the feminist movement. Creating space for the appreciation of difference, lesbian gathering, lesbian intimacy, made it possible for women to talk about 'women' without the delusion of social sameness. Without forgetting that Black women, white bourgeois women and so-called 'white trash' might all be subject to policing, deprivation, starvation, but never of quite the same kind.

The erotic takes the intellect – site of cynicism, hopelessness, fear – and overwhelms it with love, 'those physical, emotional, and psychic expressions of what is deepest and strongest and richest within each of us, being shared'. The 'low residency' course I had been teaching on did not involve much sharing; several students were suspicious of each other, spiky, allusive and aggrieved. There was not much love in the classroom and three days later it was still on my mind. I couldn't tell you for certain why the students found each other so hard to bear. All I knew was that if this classroom was a productive space, it was mostly producing resentment.

These were the thoughts that kept me company while I waited for the fresh plate of noodles, until the reverie was bluntly interrupted. A shocking realisation put an end to any thoughts of student politics, feminist theory. Somewhere, it seemed, in this chain of reflection, I had lost track of my dumpling consumption. Panic flooded my chest, my shoulders, and then my arms until even my fingernails vibrated.

What thought, I thought, could possibly have been worth my so irreversibly dropping the ball? My brain, no longer either focused or smooth, began to do something like prickle. This suggested, I suspected, sparks of early machinic malfunction. I thought I ought to get up, as though to physically exit the situation, but the last few seconds had really taken it out of me, so I stayed. I reasoned instead that, somehow, I would need to let this go. I realised, in fact, that if I didn't, the mulch in my skull might overheat. It was time to make a decision: greet the danger of 'eating too much' or feel the combustion of my own nervous system.

It was, I suppose, the first time I had properly shared any food in years.

Not counting the times I had claimed to be sharing while actually letting someone else eat for me. Like the time I went out to celebrate something at a local Indian restaurant and subjected Matt to the whole of a thali meal designed to slay a horse. I had perhaps shredded the wafer-thin edge of a dosa and bitten some fluffy lentil doughnut, coated the tines of a fork in some sauce, entertained some whisper of potato.

Unprepared to let a rare meal out go to waste, the boy embarked on a serious act of eating for two. Pausing only to comment, occasionally, on tides of pain in his stomach, he dispatched both our dinners with valour.

Assuming the degree of abdominal pain was just appropriate to the oversized meal, my surrogate eater stumbled home. There he lay curled on the bed like a sun-dried woodlouse and stayed that way for several days. By the time he was admitted to a hospital ward with what was actually a swollen appendix, his innards had responded so dramatically as to make surgical removal impossible. So long had the appendix gone untreated that the organ's neighbouring viscera had formed a protective shield. Bits of bowel and fatty membrane looped together in a mass to stop it from lethally splattering his insides. I had outsourced the wages of gluttony, letting him pay for two people's greed. Yet the pain we both took for fair punishment turned out to be something else altogether.

Over the week he spent in hospital on a drip to shrink the 'mass', I brought Matt various things. I took the bananas he had abandoned for emergency care and baked them into a cake. Mashed them with my fist and beat the pulp with sugar, tahini and oil. I mixed it with all kinds of dry stuff and scraped it into a tin, then laid over coins of the thinly sliced fruit like Jenkins had done for Elvis. I shook a thick lid of demerara sugar over the top, slammed the whole thing in the oven and waited half an hour in a thickening cloud of guilt. Sickly smells and damp, unbearable warmth filled the flat and I thought about what else I could throw at my ailing boyfriend. On the way to the hospital that afternoon, I bought a bag of those crappy jam doughnuts he sometimes liked and hoped that one of these things would redeem me. When I shuffled into the ward on the dot of visiting hour and showed him the assembled offerings, he quietly but visibly recoiled from them all. Perhaps he had had enough, I thought, of eating on my behalf, for my benefit, at my behest.

'Round two,' Matt announced, depositing the fresh pile of noodles and the cucumber on our bench. He then started to talk about some places we might spend that afternoon – parks and record stores and bars. He complained about the heat and asked if I was still hungover and kissed my head. My head was throbbing because I was, in fact, dehydrated rather than housing an overheated brain. I noticed at that moment I was strangely attuned to the words coming out of his mouth, registering the names of places he said and thinking about how we might get to them.

We were having a conversation: he would say something and I would say something back, and all this time there were dumplings and noodles and rivers of oil in the mix. I was aware of the conversation, having been forced to abandon my registry of everything I had swallowed. Shards of chilli and Sichuan pepper were stinging my nasal passage, yet still, I could sustain a basic dialogue. Barely, by now, was I thinking of mouthfuls, or tablespoons or grease or the wages of sin. I felt the whole weight of my body in the room, the hairs of his leg against my shin.

It wasn't until after that trip that I read Lorde's autobiographical novel, *Zami*, which she published in 1982. When I did, my understanding of her 'erotic' became inseparable from food.

Beginning with the author's childhood in 1930s Harlem, *Zami* charts the development of Lorde's political consciousness, which flourished in her early adulthood. Rumbling in the background is a series of sensual awakenings, sexual but culinary too. It is often, in fact, food that holds the book's women together despite a menacing divide-and-rule atmosphere in New York. 'The Rosenbergs had been executed, the transistor radio had been invented, and frontal lobotomy was the standard solution for persistent deviation. For some, Elvis Presley and his stolen Black rhythms became arch symbols of the antichrist.'

The 1950s in Greenwich Village were a time, Lorde tells us, when Black lesbian women kept their distance from each other. Often sleeping with the same white women and concealing their desires from 'the land of Black people' uptown, they saw little point, at first, in coming together as a group. It is foremost through her friendships with white lesbian women that Lorde develops a sense of sisterly love – a comradeship practised through care for one another's basic needs. 'There was always a place to sleep and something to eat and a listening ear for anyone who wandered into the crew. And there was always somebody calling you on the telephone, to interrupt the fantasies of suicide.'

Lorde tells of a Thanksgiving feast she and this loose band of friends and lovers once made for each other. Dressed in their roomiest jackets, she and a girlfriend slink across town to plunder the supermarket. They come back triumphant with a capon, two pounds of mushrooms, a box of rice and some asparagus, broken in transit. What budget they have they pour into a pint of cherry-vanilla ice cream. Requesting wine from their guests, they construct a scene of bounty and brightness from sisterly teamwork. Whether the goods involved are purchased, gifted or pinched, their procurement is an organised business.

It is only when Lorde begins to discover parties that food becomes a source of potential anxiety. Parties given by Black women, she finds, are 'always full of food and dancing and reefer and laughter and high-jinks'. It is here that she learns to move with voices and music, to feel the common throb of a room. White women's parties are different. The music isn't easy to dance to. There is wine but no hard liquor and never enough food.

We're talking little plates of crisps, and crackers and dips, 'tiny little jars of red caviar with bright green bibs around them', saucers of raw vegetables just at the edges of tables and nibble-able offerings, like nuts. Lorde sees this dainty non-dinner and dreams of the potato salad, hot corn bread and abundant chicken wings she remembers from parties elsewhere. It is as though the expensive parsimony sprinkled about the room can account for its limp, disjointed feel. 'Mostly, women sat around in little groups and talking quietly, the sound of moderation – thick and heavy as smoke in the air.'

In one of the book's final scenes, Lorde finds inspiration at a lesbian party in Queens. Here the liquor flows viscous and heavy: gin bourbon, scotch and various mixers stand opened, the bar less dotted than swamped with delicacies of all descriptions. Most important, there is a platter of fried chicken wings, a pan of potato-and-egg salad dressed with vinegar, a huge central platter of beef arranged over a pan of cracked ice. The room is 'alive and pulsing with loud music, good food and beautiful Black women in all different combinations of dress'.

For Lorde, to feast is not to revel in the privilege of rarefied food. *This internal requirement toward excellence*

*we learn from the erotic must not be misconstrued as demand-
ing the impossible from ourselves nor from others.* Her problem
with the white women's parties is not a lack of generosity
with money – caviar, after all, costs more than chicken. It is
more, it seems, the lack of sensuality available from garnish-
adjacent food – food to be picked at discreetly, its effect on
the body unacknowledged, unshared. The problem is that
this sensual void drains a party's potential to make anything
meaningful happen. The hot bulk of cornbread, a heap of
dressed potatoes – these are offerings that demand to be felt,
to be eaten with the full participation of dancing arms, necks,
shoulders and bellies. If a 'better and more beautiful food'
appeals to Lorde in the company of women, it is a food that is
well within her reach – food with the capacity to turn a mere
guest-list of names into a synchronous, breathing crowd.

Big, unignorable, shareable, more-than-enough-for-
everyone food need not demand your gratitude. It need not
demand your mindfulness or carefulness with 'waste', your
gestures of privilege-awareness. What the chicken and beef
and cornbread and potatoes bring to *Zami* is a scene that
mirrors the scene of friendship – a place in which there is
always something to eat, a listening ear, a place to sleep. The
best of the parties Lorde describes don't just nourish their
guests – they install an *expectation* of abundance. The erotic,
Lorde would later write, is 'an internal sense of satisfaction
to which, once we have experienced it, we know we can
aspire. For having experienced the fullness of this depth of
feeling and recognizing its power, in honor and self-respect
we can require no less of ourselves.'

What does it mean to require of yourself a kind of
pleasure that society has never been willing to give you? It

cannot mean being prepared to burgle corner shops all your life, or counting only parties – fleeting micro-worlds – as life. In 'Learning from the 60s', Lorde writes of the unequal distribution of food as a thoroughly political issue. Decisions to cut food stamps and school lunches, she wrote, were being made by 'men with full stomachs who live in comfortable houses with two cars and umpteen tax shelters'. These were men who had never known hunger, just as many who were hungry rarely had the means to know joy. If joy was to awaken the hungry to anticipate more for themselves, this 'more' would then need to be made into a solid political demand.

All those who had been robbed of their right to eat, Lorde implied, now urgently needed to join in demanding that their stomachs be filled. For the greatest use of the erotic, that seemingly most private of things, is in fact entirely public. For feasting to be truly political, for desire to be politically productive, it has to be more than simply eating to the point of thinking, *How lucky I am!* It must surely mean eating to the point at which a scarcity mindset no longer feels possible. It must surely mean eating to the point of thinking, *This is how it should always be, for everyone who wants it, many times a day.* It is eating to the point of refusing to bear the fact that this isn't the case. *Who has access to this feeling already?* we might ask. *Who doesn't and why is that? What can be done to ensure that things are different as soon as they possibly can be?* Lorde believes that the 1960s should teach us '[h]ow important it is not to allow our leaders to define ourselves to ourselves, or to define our sources of power to us'. We are told that we each have it in us to make the best of how things are. But what if, as more than individuals, our power is to make something else of this world?

The use of erotic communion is to acclimatise those who feel it to a moment of abundance so urgent it demands to be made a permanent fixture of social life. For Lorde this meant picketing in throngs, lobbying in groups, canvassing in squadrons for the kind of world that would make sure all of its denizens were nourished. Though the action of *Zami* is propelled by small acts of sisterhood – hosting, borrowing, theft – its horizon is a world where you wouldn't have to count your chicken wings or ask or look around or be grateful. Instead, you would simply go about your life expecting to be able to eat.

The more I enjoyed those dumplings, the more my thoughts became fixed on some dal I hadn't been able to enjoy. The spiced vat of lentils I had smelled at a meeting after a Metropolitan policeman kidnapped, raped and murdered a young woman. I was chairing the women's branch of my local constituency Labour Party in South London, and felt I should organise something for members in response. Beyond this 'something', however, I felt no inspiration, no confidence, resourcefulness or hope. I had no more concrete a sense of what to do than a sense of whether anything was worth it.

The feminist direct action group Sisters Uncut were holding gatherings in other parts of London. Their aim was to empower local people against the more violent arm of the state. On a very cold night I schlepped across town in a vague gesture of something. I hoped, I suppose, I would connect with some Sisters who could advise, or even help me in my task. Could tell me how to step, like someone sentient and wise, into the role I had once willingly stood for. The meeting's leaders, sure enough, were welcoming, self-assured and loud. They came with a hotplate and bowls. But I was not in the business of welcoming unexpected food.

So deep was my fear of such things, in fact, that it is hard to say which I admired more: that certain people looked prepared to kick a cop in the side of the head or that they were able to eat a bowl of dal. There was no performative pleasure in their embrace of the steaming, thick dinner, no theatrics of eating-as-transgression. The eating was fundamental to the proceedings, to why we were there, but it was nothing like the point. We were not there to overstate the value of eating as self-love, as though this were the ultimate feminist achievement. We were there for group discussion, education, organisation, and for that, it was assumed, we should be fed. We were there to feed each other's interest and belief in making a London less threatening to women, whether the threat be malnourishment by the capitalist state or strangulation by its police.

I admired these dal-wielding Sisters, but didn't believe I could be them. I left, and left the work to those who saw no time for despair.

I wonder, when I think of such moments, how much my faithless disposition might have been softened by a slug of warming stew. I suspect I hoped it was enough to let the smell of it fill my clothes, like a kind of communal perfume just as bonding as a feast. I wonder if it would have been such a stretch just to let it on my tongue – let it fill my facial cavities like the sting of fierce garlic would fill my whole sensorium that New York afternoon, the one when I forgot to count my dumplings. What if I had let the spices churn in my blood until they leaked out through my sweat and onto the pavement? Why was it only on the Lower East Side that I was ready to let go, with nobody but Matt to smell my sweat? How frustrating that it was only in a restaurant, such an anti-political space, that I would incriminate my body with desire.

I had not gone to that part of Chinatown for anything related to a profound experience of sisterhood. I had simply gone to eat lunch, and though it took some mental detours this was, in the end, what I achieved.

But maybe I also achieved, that mealtime, a small sense of what could have been. In fact, I achieved the very thought: 'I wonder how much my faithless disposition might have been softened by a slug of warming stew at that meeting?' What might have happened, in the last few years of half-arsed attempts at being a person, had I allowed myself to share the experience of food in settings less incidental? Settings fuller with purpose, perhaps, more *charged* with political will?

It is perhaps unfair to suggest that a restaurant could never be such a place. According to historian Alex Ketchum, who wrote a long book on the topic of feminist cafés, the first known feminist restaurant to grace the USA opened in 1972 in Greenwich Village. Walking distance, in fact, from my dumpling experience. Mother Courage was founded by feminist activists Dolores Alexander and Jill Ward, a pair whose political partnership grew from erotic connection. The duo were romantic partners, in the literal sense, but they were also sharers of food – that source of internal satisfaction that teaches us how to aspire.

The idea for this restaurant was born from a moment of political disenchantment, coinciding with a late-night craving for spaghetti and meatballs. Alexander had recently stepped down as executive director of the National Organization for Women on the grounds of anti-lesbian sentiment. Ward, too, had just left her job, and was looking for new fulfilment in her life as a feminist activist. The thought, 'we should open a spaghetti house', turned into the designing of a place for women to meet. A place where feminist lesbians and their friends could mix openly, organise politically, eat well.

The restaurant had been funded with crowd-sourced micro-loans and personal savings. Its construction was the work of friends and family. In some people's eyes, this alone might be enough to make the project a 'feminist' endeavour, given that women had next to no access to business investment at the time. But a restaurant alone, whatever its provenance or organisational structure, was not enough to satisfy Alexander's vision of feminist action. In an oral history project from 2004–5 recalling her life and achievements, she talks of separately seeking out the New York Radical Feminist group, organising speakouts on marriage and work.

It was the restaurant, however, that would end up giving those women both a place to meet and an activity – decent eating – through which to connect. They were mostly lesbians who lived in the Village, and part of what made their work so effective, in Alexander's opinion, was their 'proximity' and mutual understanding. 'We wanted to be a space', she said, 'for strong, independent women who would hopefully be involved in the women's movement, and that did happen.' After a while, women came from all over the world to eat at Mother Courage. A destination made of a cheaply renovated luncheonette with sketches on walls, lit up by surplus streetlamps.

Among the regulars amassed from New York's feminist literary circles was none other than Audre Lorde. On learning this, I wondered what she would have made of their 'freshest food available, simply and deliciously prepared'. Archived menus under this strapline include, of course, spaghetti and meatballs, but also a number of other big-hitting mains, very often described as 'smothered in butter'. Sauces are 'creamy and rich', chickens stuffed with mozzarella and one dish is 'strictly for garlic lovers'. Reviews of the food were mixed. In *New York* magazine, Linda Wolfe described the main course offerings as 'chancy'. The veal marsala, for example, was 'cloyingly sweet', the veal Garibaldi 'too salty'. But if these gripes converge on anything, it is nothing but *too much flavour*. The food is clearly unstinting, with spinach and mushroom salad 'bedecked with more crisp bacon than at most places'. The Greek salad 'does not skimp on feta cheese' and the stroganoff comes 'mighty with mushrooms'. It is hard to separate this kind of generosity from the spirit of the socialist feminist project, founded on the principle of *more than enough to go round*.

This is not, however, the principle that organises life in capitalist society at large. Mother Courage tried to pay its staff well and feed its guests at a reasonable price, but this was not the plan the US economic system had in mind for female small business owners. 'Obviously', said Ward and Alexander, 'to survive we all had to compromise to some degree.' Hence the name 'Mother Courage', a character created by the playwright Bertolt Brecht. Mother Courage is both a victim of the seventeenth century's Thirty Years' War and a woman canny enough to exploit it. 'Like the war to nourish you?' a sergeant taunts her in the play's first act. 'Have to feed it something too.' Brecht's Mother Courage makes her living selling extortionate provisions to soldiers. Ward and Alexander weren't extortionate, but they had to exploit themselves.

Ward and Alexander overworked themselves for six years – feeding women's anti-capitalist meetings while trying to run a business. They cooked despite the fact that this was merely a break-even operation. They cooked despite a hostile world outdoors and the heat and bad tips and no financial support.

This is what they tried to do right up until they didn't. By the end of Brecht's play Mother Courage is a mother no more – she has lost all three of her children to relentlessly grim conditions. One day in 1977, Ward left a note on the restaurant's front door: 'Sorry folks, I just can't do it anymore.' According to Ketchum, most feminist restaurants followed a similar trajectory, finding popularity but closing nonetheless for reasons of money, disagreement or exhaustion. New restaurants opened up, and the political plans that were made in them long outlived each business. The question remains, however, of how to sustain collective space. How to uphold erotic communion when the governing economic logic wants to privatise every opportunity for it? Perhaps we must begin by simply scavenging the feeling wherever we can.

'You gonna eat that?' said Matt, jabbing a dripping chopstick at the final dumpling.

'I know,' I said, having slightly but fundamentally misheard. 'You can eat that' is what I thought he had said, which had I been less on the defensive I might have heard as a selfless gesture. *You can eat that, since I am willing to make a sacrifice for you. I will forgo the final dumpling since we're sharing and*

I want it but I think you might want it too. Instead, what I heard was 'you can eat that' as an exasperated statement. *I know you think you can't, but you can eat that since eating isn't actually all that hard.* It was the kind of condescension I had come to expect from eating disorder treatment, but one that had been given new meaning. If only for thirty seconds of absorption in ideas and people beyond myself, I had eaten without even thinking, as though it were easy after all. It had been easy to eat, but not because a doctor or therapist was telling me so. It had been easy, just briefly, thanks to an almost-erotic absorption in Audre Lorde's *use of the erotic.*

'You gonna eat that?' Such a total non-question, to be heard and then forgotten as soon as answered and acted upon. Such a total non-question and a total non-scene of two people eating chain-restaurant dumplings. But I heard 'you can eat that' and will always hear it now when I remember this non-event. Remember having an inkling of what it might mean to treat a meal as no big deal. Expertly made and generous, perhaps, but also nothing more than what a meal should always be. Better and more beautiful than nothing, but not so unattainable as Christ. I heard the wrong thing and now I hear it again, and I hope I will hear it again if ever I too get the feeling I can't do it any more.

4

You Feed

That summer many people attempted to tempt me to eat. I had not been expecting, when the summer turned cold, the invitation to cook.

I laughed at first, a volley of voice-notes flying through my phone. They came from the mother of a good, but now unfamiliar, childhood friend. She spoke at me with a lately unfamiliar kind of respect, as though I were the kind of person who could be trusted with things like dinner.

She explained that she had been planning a 'sacred happening' for some of her healing clients – a retreat to the edge of Wales where those who took part could expect to connect with their souls. She was offering me a deal, whereby if I came and took care of the food, I could be part of the healing circle without suffering the fee. I would stay in a house energetically charged with decades of Tibetan meditation in return for my provision of 'delicious plant food with a basis in Eastern flavours'. Following a string of unfortunate let-downs by other would-be cooks, this mother from the past had been struck by a sudden, but firm conviction: that she might in fact be messaging the Best Cook in the World.

'Have a think and let me know,' she said, 'because I think perhaps this was meant to be. *You* are meant to come and help us with your cooking and not those other people.'

'Intuitively,' she continued in a separate note, which landed a few minutes later, 'I feel very strongly that you actually need to be there.' She laughed a laugh of what might have been desperation to staff her event, but couldn't be ruled out as a laugh of hard warning against the denial of my fate.

For reasons unknown, I sensed that the mother from the past was right about this. That I was, indeed, The One to cater her healing venture, all these years since I'd known her at school. I wondered if it was nostalgia fuelling this bout of unlikely trust, then remembered that I'd hated my schooldays.

I laughed because anyone closely involved in my life would have thought the proposition deranged: to summon a woman actively failing to feed herself to oversee the feeding of others. Beware, we have been told, the woman who cooks and never stops to eat, who fills her hands with goodies to thrust into your mouth until there's nothing left to put into her own. Probably trying to poison you with caramel and fat in some sick biological war, sacrificing you to her project of clutching at the means of 'control'. Somebody who did not love me might put it this way. Others converted the equation of concern into a matter of my own wellbeing. 'Sounds nuts,' was someone's opinion. 'Sounds like a very bad idea. How can you go around feeding when you can't even care for yourself?'

This did not seem to be the impression held by the mother from the past. 'This feels to me', she said, 'like an important time for healing in your life.' Cooking for the benefit of others, she implied, was compatible with my wellbeing. Conducive, even, to repairing whatever it was that needed repair.

Not that I was entirely unsuspicious of this take. Keeping the retreaters alive was not, I noted, a well-remunerated job. Was it now my turn to shoulder the kind of thankless motherly tasks that had kept me in fish fingers after school? To re-enact the pleasure in providing I had expected, as a child, from this mother, as well as from my own?

Nor was I unselfconscious about the strangeness of the gap between my readiness to feed and to eat. I had always cooked with an energy that rushed to overshoot the threshold of people's mere fullness. Meanness had always seemed to me the most appalling thing – to have skimped, underseasoned, underfed. It sometimes felt like my life's work to eliminate this risk when it came to the feeding of others, and still, I had arrived at a state where I committed this crime against myself daily.

But maybe this only seemed odd because 'crime', like feeding, is an active capacity – a deed. Failing to eat, meanwhile, seemed more like the opposite of something you do. Living in a state of hunger was an absence of sorts: of the strength to get involved, look alive. I still believed – who doesn't? – in everyone's right to eat; I had just lost the will to claim it for myself. Optimism of the intellect, pessimism of the will, a Gramscian motto in reverse. Feeding without eating was a limbo space between hope and private despair – a respect for others' idea that the world might be redeemed, coexisting with my own reluctance to wait around to find out.

It must have been the intellect, then, and not the pessimistic will, that made me like the idea of a 'happening'. I imagined a noisy homage to 1960s theatrics – free concerts in the park where Janis Joplin played and people set fire to money. Sometimes the food at these happenings was the happening itself – the thing that happened was feeding. I knew that such events had been fed by artists like Diane di Prima – the bushy-haired anarchist poet who seemed to be everywhere now. She had died in 2020 and a blood-red collection of her *Revolutionary Letters* had been published in her wake. She had apparently mailed these poems back and forth to Audre Lorde, a childhood friend and adult comrade. In the collection's introduction, the writer Sophie Lewis had observed that the letters still made the rounds 'in moments of heightened struggle and dispiriting defeat'. I read them in an afternoon. They were practical and chaotic, fun and full of food. Maybe I could channel that.

Di Prima did not give me the impression of a 'feeder' to be held in suspicion. After excusing herself from college to experiment with communal living in 1950s New York, she grew herself a reputation as a provider of food and shelter for friends, poets, musicians, homeless comrades, hangers-on. She had seen her anarchist grandfather Domenico Mallozzi routinely bring home unjustly treated co-workers and their families, feeding and housing them, giving them a shove to consider fighting their case through a union. Decades later, pouring soup for activists at her own revolutionary table, di Prima would thank Mallozzi, in an 'April Fool Birthday Poem for Grandpa', for educating her in the love that 'you told us had to come or we / die'. Her own idea of warding off this premature death was showing radicals of various kinds how to provide for one another's bodies. Her 'Revolutionary Letter #3' offered in verse a survival recipe for fugitives and those who hid them: a full bathtub, measures of brown rice, flour and beans, fruit, nuts, salt and oil.

These revolutionary letters, written from 1968 and throughout the rest of di Prima's life, were a creative call to action. Printed in free newspapers and shouted from the steps of San Francisco City Hall, they coincided with di Prima's move west. She had seen in the flowering counterculture a chance to translate her own communal remaking of homes into an organised remaking of cities. In San Francisco in 1966, she joined the anti-capitalist Diggers – an experimental theatre troupe-cum-mutual aid movement – to organise happenings and 'be ins'. Central to these was the scavenging and distribution of free food, which di Prima and her household also hand-delivered twice a week to twenty-five urban communes. The top of di Prima's fridge was home to the Diggers' Free Bank – a shoebox full of money for whoever felt they needed it. The Diggers tuned into a wider recruitment of food to political purposes – fasts against the Vietnam War, sit-ins at racially segregated restaurants, grape and lettuce boycotts in support of agricultural workers – and believed that 'every brother should have what he needs to do his thing'.

This premise was grounded in a spiritual flight from mainstream American thought. The Diggers were spooked by the Western landscape of human consuming machines – rugged individuals jostling for slices of chemically seasoned pie. They turned instead to Buddhist notions of dharmic interdependence, the idea that all things, experiences and therefore people are connected. This was precisely the kind of enchantment with Eastern ideals that attracted di Prima to them, following years of Zen practice, some spells on LSD and a studentship of the hidden religions.

Though later, in her 2001 autobiography *Recollections of My Life as a Woman*, di Prima would acknowledge the awkwardness of Westerners despoiling Eastern traditions, talking down her own youthful tendency to mix religious metaphors, the point was not to fetishise 'tradition', but to attend to what specific traditions could achieve. Combining Tibetan Buddhism with Western mystic traditions – alchemy, Gnosticism, Tarot – di Prima sought ideals and principles suited to shaping revolutionary struggle. This struggle would not be won by guns, she predicted in 'Revolutionary Letter #7'. Gun warfare was merely a tactic. Di Prima was interested in strategies – ideas about how to see through the long process of change. Di Prima advised that what would 'win' in the strategic sense would be 'mantras, the sustenance we give each other, the energy we plug into / (the fact that we touch / share food)'.

As with my reunion with the mother from the past, di Prima's spiritual awakening came to her almost by mistake. She had been searching for someone to officiate her marriage to her 'gay hustler' actor friend Alan Marlowe. Anarchists both, without a rabbi or a priest to bind them together, the couple were introduced to Shunryu Suzuki Roshi, a Zen master freshly arrived in New York from a stint in San Francisco. Despite di Prima's aversion to the idea of any guru – a notion she dismissed as 'romantic' – Suzuki provoked in her an instantaneous, bodily trust. There was a nakedness, she felt, to his presence, his gaze unconcealed and deep. She sensed he saw both into and through her, not only inspiring immediate faith, but making himself, by virtue of this novel inspiration, her teacher by default.

★

I did not know, when I decided I was destined to cook for the mother from the past and her guests, exactly what it was that drew me. I did not know what it was, exactly, that I thought was going to 'happen'. This was something her PDF flyer seemed to leave open by design. As a guest, I was promised the retreat would meet me wherever I was in life and carry me, on a tide of mantras, meditations, yoga and gongs, wherever I wanted to be.

It was hard to imagine what kind of food should accompany such a transition. Had I truly wanted to channel di Prima I might have subjected the assembled crowd to a week's worth of brown rice variations. In 1963, the 'festive' New Year's Day meal she cooked for friends was built around three consecutive courses of the unrefined grain. *Dashi-no-moto*, the Japanese instant soup, with rice and a crumble of seaweed; eggy croquettes reconstructed from yesterday's rice with hot brown rice on the side, and finally a brown rice pudding with cinnamon, tahini and raisins.

Like many of the counterculture's children, di Prima was the faithful practitioner of a Zen macrobiotic diet. Inspired by the culinary habits of Edo-era Japan, i.e. before the country's Westernisation, the macrobiotic lifestyle was aimed at reincarnating health in the land of mass-produced cow patties. Resisting the lure of plastic ice-cream and chemically fertilised fruit, followers of macrobiotics stuck to local, organic meals composed for the most part of vegetables and grains. Layered onto this broader refusal of industrialised products were ideas adapted from Taoist philosophy – specifically a set of meticulous instructions for how to negotiate the yin and yang that flowed from different foods.

In Taoist thought, and other Chinese traditions that preceded it, yin-yang is a law of the universe, the ultimate cause of life and death. It describes the interaction of forces that, when in balance, produce health, and when imbalanced, produce its opposite. The implications of these principles for diet are intricate and complex, involving endlessly moving parts. Fish who live in chilly, yin environments must eat plenty of yang algae to ward off the cold. A human must respond to the shifting intensity of forces in their body and environment to ward off disease. They must incorporate yang in their diets if they are going to create new life, but also yin if they are going to support growth. They must balance the yin in what they eat with the yang *qi*, or energy, within them. The Zen macrobiotic diet pioneered in the West by George Ohsawa all but gutted these terms, lumping them into a basic set of rules for things you should and shouldn't eat.

'Absolutely avoid the most Yin vegetables,' reads Ohsawa's 1965 guide to the diet: 'potatoes, tomatoes and eggplant.' Anything puffed with baking soda was similarly much too yin. This diet, which in its purest version consisted only of plain brown rice and was more than once accused of killing its adherents, didn't much inspire me to cook. I had never much been interested in health, or, contrary to stereotypes of anorectic religiosity, in seemingly arbitrary prohibitions.

Yet it did seem that something in macrobiotics had been healing for di Prima. At the time when she discovered the diet, everything she ate seemed to be causing her pain and diarrhoea, leading her to suspect that years of pastries dunked in amphetamine-spiked coffee had finally wrecked her insides. When her friend Billy Linch came to tend to her,

cooking her macrobiotic food, she found in whole grains, seaweeds, salt plums and ginger tea a gastric balm from the blue. As the Food and Drug Administration raided health food stores, spraying these suspect hippie goods with pesticide, di Prima grew a conviction that the body of the eater knows better than the Feds. 'The food felt good inside of me,' she wrote in *Recollections*; 'I could digest it, I knew that much.'

It appears that what was healing for di Prima was less the specific foods she ate than the act of responding to principles that felt, to her, true. Ohsawa's list of prescriptions has an almost scriptural feel, yet in di Prima's case it was not the commandments of required and prohibited foods that seemed to intrigue or inspire her change of diet. Rather, the philosophy that underlay these rules – her faith in the value of balance. Di Prima recognised that in Taoist tradition, both yin and the yang forces had their place – the spiritual and the worldly, the soulful and the egoic, the inwardly and outwardly nourishing. The idea that one might live by such principles through everyday things like food was a source of unexpected energy. 'I began to look', she wrote, 'for the structures on which I could hang my own experience, my knowledge. The principle(s) that could shape and inform my Will.'

If 'Revolutionary Letter #41' is anything to go by, di Prima found in the notion of necessary balance a cosmic ground for faith in the certainty of change. Revolution, she wrote, was a turning like the earth among planets and the sun among stars. It described 'a yin/yang spiral in the aether', a turn from dark to light.

I was not myself inclined to wait for this revolutionary faith to emerge before I could start planning meals. It would have been good to be able to plan from a place of un-complex

enthusiasm for food; not to have had to ask myself of every dreamt-up meal how much of it I thought I could eat. But practicality called, so I went ahead and thought about what I was capable of cooking in bulk; what I could make to a useful extent in advance. What I could see myself handling serenely in a kitchen with undisclosed equipment. What people would find familiar without being so banal that it killed the healing vibe. I was haunted by one summer holiday in which I had had to persuade a friend, floating high on a cloud of acid, to come inside and eat lasagne with our very patient host. '*Lasagne?!*' he had shrieked, as though he were watching the birth of his own child and I'd asked him to come and watch *Friends*. Some things are simply too earthly for the spiritual plane.

I wrote down a list of suggestions and sent them over to the mother from the past. I tried to tread a line between warm hippy slop and sense-awakening novelty. Coconut dal to mix with rice, and mop with buttery flatbreads; Indonesian salads, sticky with nuggets of tempeh and sour peanut dressing; piles of oven-crunchy yin potatoes for luck and beans for every mood. Deep pots of aubergine and walnut stew, darkened with olive oil. The mother told me she liked to keep it 'healthy' between meals, serving rice cakes and plates of fresh fruit. She didn't refuse my suggestions, though, for after-dinner sweets: slabs of apple and pistachio tart, chocolate and olive oil cakes, rose and semolina pastries.

I loaded all the elements into her car – cool-bags wedged between yoga mats and vegetables perched on gongs. I also brought my copies of di Prima's *Revolutionary Letters*, *Recollections of My Life as a Woman* and her ominously titled *Dinners and Nightmares*. I braced myself in the passenger seat

to reacquaint with the mother, inching as we were out of London in the general direction of Wales.

It was only then that she asked me what I needed to heal. I didn't like to say it was she who had seemed to think this retreat was something I needed; that maybe she could tell *me*. The obvious answer, had I not been about to cook for all her guests, might have been 'my eating disorder', but even then, it wouldn't quite have been true that this was what made me suffer. Anorexia seemed to me more like a symptom than a problem of its own, mere pus from the originating wound.

I said that I'd been feeling kind of useless and that this made me kind of depressed, which seemed to be turning my uselessness kind of chronic. Every morning I'd consider the things people do to try and be part of this world and every evening I observed I hadn't done them.

The mother from the past observed that it was clearly important to me to carry out caring work. That maybe this was why I needed to come and cook for her retreat.

That night, before any guests arrived, the mother cooked for me. After battling with an ancient gas oven – huge but outstandingly weak – she pulled out some lemongrass tofu and served it with limey glass noodles and scoops of warm mung bean mush. The mother from the past, three years a grandmother now, returned us to the question of care. As I ate, she asked me if I wanted a child. Someone else to look after, she expanded, something to fill up my days and give me the sense of a reason to exist.

Here we go, I thought: the ultimate bourgeois cure for melancholy – the go-to solution for a lack of political will; to harness all that energy you wished you could direct at

building a world in common and pouring it all instead into your own nuclear household. I reached for my routine defences, the most diplomatic first, against her impossible question:

'I don't really have any money,' I said, as though no un-rich child had ever been born. 'I don't really have any space. My flat is just one room,' as though any infant were the size of a room. 'I don't have housing security or paid maternity leave,' as though any writer does. 'I haven't menstruated in years' was something I didn't say, but I knew that was irrelevant too. No doctor was saying I *couldn't* menstruate one day, should I wish to change my life. The mother from the past was unconvinced that I'd actually answered her question.

The mother from the past advised that if I *did* want a child I should ask my angels to take care of the details. She told me that if it was for my highest good, the smaller things would sort themselves out. She cut me a radioactive-looking swirl of pandan cake that melted into sugar before I could even chew.

I raised the stakes, heightened the tone of my defence. What if my having a child wasn't for anybody's good? What if there were already people enough on this already too-hot earth? I knew this was a disingenuous way to look concerned for the good of humankind – the kind of thing nativists said when they wanted to stop Black and brown people repro-ducing; the kind of thing oil conglomerates said when they wanted to shift the blame. I knew that it would make more sense to think about how the world's resources were used than to start from a place of whittling down the number of people who used them. Still, I had learnt over time that to talk about children this way – as a kind of environmental pollutant – was surprisingly persuasive to many of the people who brought them up, a reliable way to shut down the conversation I didn't want to have.

What I could not say – no more easily to myself than to others – was that having a child felt like daring to hope for something that might not come. By this I did not mean fertility, financial security or space, but a future worth being born into.

What I also could not say, since it would have been untrue, was that I did not want a child. That the thought did not provoke in me a pleasant kind of ache for what could be, were I a person who hoped.

In truth, it may have only been the intellect that drew me to di Prima's legacy as a feeder of comrades and communes, but it was probably something more like the will – like my desire – that absorbed me in her writing on motherhood. Di Prima did not hold herself hostage to caveats such as mine when it came to the question of reproducing. Despite no money, room of her own or salaried job with leave and benefits, she found herself feeling one day that if she didn't have a baby, she was 'going to get sick'. She did not know how it would work to incorporate an infant into her life of poetry and study, theatre and friends, but then, she thought, she hadn't known how those things would work or come about until they did: 'I was thoroughly of the opinion', she wrote, 'that the only way to find out if the angels would bear you up was to make the leap.'

Di Prima allowed herself to want to give birth without caving in, in the process, to the state's idea of a Mother – a woman legally conscripted to the single-minded service of her husband and his biological brood. At fourteen, when she decided she was going to live in looser, more sprawling kinds of kinship arrangements, she soberly noted the things she would likely have to go without: 'the quiet unquestioned living and dying . . . material pleasures, easy securities. I am leaving the houses I will never own. Dishwashers. Carpets.' Carpets and dishwashers mattered, di Prima felt in that moment, and yet she had seen the whole package for the 'prison' that it was. 'Every woman a political prisoner,' she wrote in 'Revolutionary Letter #49'. 'Every woman a political prisoner.'

A woman is a capital-M Mother, for society and state, the moment she produces a child. It does not take a woman, however, to mother as a verb. Di Prima learnt to mother from her grandfather and did it every day of her life, before she ever was pregnant and after her children were parents themselves. She mothered those who drifted in her orbit and knew that she'd be mothered in return – by Linch and the macro community, by 'wondrous girl-cousins' who cleaned and fed her children while she wrote and translated medieval Latin.

This began with the 'extended family' she developed in New York, in a thirty-three-dollar-a-month apartment. 'No telling how many of us would pile in together,' she wrote in *Recollections*, 'especially in the winter. Or shared the cash, whose-even it was, the food, whatever it might be.' Di Prima made this rolling clan breakfasts of oatmeal and dinners of rice and beans. She welcomed gifts of bread, wine, coffee and fuel from whoever was able to gift it. A skilful home economist, inspired by herself and ruled by nothing and no one, di Prima knew the price of butter. Chicken gizzards were nineteen cents a pound, eggs twenty-nine cents a dozen and cream-cheese-on-datenut-bread sandwiches twenty cents from Chock Full O'Nuts. Toilet paper came from public bathrooms, electricity was pirated from the hall. People mothered one another however they liked and could.

What need, in such a hive of familial love, to reproduce your own genetic matter? Why should a feminist like di Prima be bothered with the 'call' to make a child with her body? Perhaps, to use the words of French philosopher Hélène Cixous, because 'either you want a kid or you don't'. Of wanting a child, di Prima describes a visceral 'fullness' straining inside her body, 'as if there were more of me than I needed or could use in myself'. As if there were something inside that 'needed to grow into another'.

To grow another human, for di Prima, was merely one among many ways you might make use of your love. Whether or not this was your thing, she hoped that it might be everyone's to care about children in general. For di Prima, 'No child is hungry who is not your grandchild . . . no child is orphaned who is not your son.' She may have learnt something of love from the 'joyful', 'opening', 'unconquerable' act of giving birth, and yet to extend this love to those who did not share her blood was always, it seemed, the point.

In California, di Prima found herself in the company of like-minded women – women who 'gave their love where they wished'. In San Francisco, single mothers nursed their babies in the sun as other adults kept an eye on the many other children. Motherly duties were shared in the manner of good California wine, which, not just due to its cheapness, flowed freely. People were shared in the manner of the figs and plums they snaffled from orchards that had no owner.

These principles of sharing were basic to the work of the California Diggers, who dreamt of a classless society where food was abundant for all. Where a city made of nuclear families seemed like a city of competitive teams, beavering for nothing but their own relative comfort, the Diggers aspired to forge 'Free Cities', composed of 'Free Families' working for each other: Diggers, Black Panthers, Provos, 'revolutionist gangs' and communes. According to a Digger broadside, the idea was to set up services that would allow these groups to work 'without having to hassle for food'. Or money, transportation, housing, clothes, space to work, or machines to print their credos.

The vision was of a 'hip food network' of communes, each with gardeners and nearby farms. To get things going, the Diggers tried to model this utopia themselves. The sharing of food required for this disburdening scheme was a burden for Digger members. Volunteers were instructed to 'beg, borrow, steal and form liaisons' to hijack every available source of free food – markets, farms, dairies, ranches, packing plants and overfed institutions. Once loaded up with bread, salad, turkey stew and apples, they would dream up ways to convince the people of San Francisco that this food was 'free because it's yours'. They'd show up in parks, or at organised conventions, or drive to communal homes. They'd set up 'free stores' where if you asked to see the manager, they'd tell you that was you.

'TODAY IS THE FIRST DAY OF THE REST OF YOUR LIFE' reads one of the *Digger Papers*, collectively produced publications through which the group would spread their word:

Free food

Lion meat
Soul vegetables
Blue chip dairy goods

Everymorning delivered to
Your commune.

Fresh fish
Ripe fruit
Solid greens

Everyevening feed the brothers
And sisters in your house.

Late on Monday morning, hours into the first day of the rest of my life, my brothers and sisters, or children, arrived in Wales. Since I was, in a sense, to give them everything they needed to do their thing, I was keen to discover just what these things were. Among the group, there were many who were just as confused as I was – just as unsure of what they wanted from this place. Others, though, were surer and – much to my unease – proportionately unsettling.

Abraham the accountant comes to memory first. He had a voice engineered to fill a showroom and was not much into meditation, but knew he liked to spend time with the mother from the past. More typical was Sadie, who identified as a 'founder' and came with a special concern for her 'attentional performance'. Sadie was irritated that something, possibly some trauma from her childhood, was making it harder for her to concentrate in meetings. If seven days harnessing the power of the breath could help her 'augment her mental delivery', she thought this probably sounded worth pursuing. Milo wanted a girlfriend, a freehold and a dog, ideally in that order. He sensed some kind of blockage to his manifestation of these things. Milo was pleased to be in Wales in the company of similarly aspirational people; he suspected part of the blockage might be down to the 'riff raff' overrunning his meditation class at the gym.

We seemed on course for the kind of happening organised by a corporate human resources department – one less creative than *productive*, less to do with the kind of raised consciousness that might alter human relations than the kind of 'raised alertness' that changes nothing but the self. That night when I withdrew to the kitchen to start swirling oil around pans, I feared I might be oiling something bad. I feared I might have agreed to lubricate the already well-greased wheels of libertarian smugness. Flinging a fistful of mustard seeds into the shallows of fat I watched as they spat with disapproval. I think I'd hoped to find that modern spirituality, even when packaged for sale, could somehow be retrieved from a crassly individualist culture. I'd hoped to be disabused of my sense of an unbreachable rift between political advance and therapeutic retreat.

Here I was instead, playing mother to something I wasn't sure I wanted to birth. At dinner, the property owners whose lists of things owned included properties they didn't live in swapped tales of the insufferable tenants who paid their mortgages for them. Everyone, though perhaps for different reasons, laughed at the story of the 'kleptomaniac' evictee who stole a kitchen sink. It was debated whether disrespecting recently decorated walls ought to make you a candidate for homelessness.

I developed a concern that my feeding duties in this setting might end up having less to do with care than with 'taking a cop to dinner'. When, in 1960s San Francisco, hippie-centric premises were daily subjected to drug busts, health food stores and psychedelic shops put signs in their unbroken windows urging their clientele to be hospitable to the cops. They seemed to want to demonstrate that hippies, rather than a menace to the police, were generous, non-violent citizens. The Diggers, unimpressed, wrote a broadside warning their readers to watch who you feed. To take a cop to dinner with payoffs, freebies, tickets, discounts and drinks, feeding the image of the less-than-menacing neighbourhood policeman, was tantamount, they thought, to feeding state violence itself. 'Take a cop to dinner this week,' the Diggers dared, 'and feed his power to judge, prosecute and brutalize the streets of your city.'

I wouldn't have put my own misgivings so strongly, but I did begin to wonder just what I'd agreed to do. I wondered how I might still achieve that thing – whatever the thing was – that I had wanted to happen that week. It seemed the thing to do was most probably to maintain trust in the mother from the past. Leap and expect the reality to prove itself richer than my own, unimaginative, fears.

I suppose I could also have poisoned them all; met the prevailing expectations of an anorexic witch. For ever since we made it women's role to feed other people with love, we have also felt it our duty to suspect them of feeding to kill. There will always be some, we calculate, inclined to object to their designated nurturant role. Perhaps, after all, this is not so unreasonable a thing for a woman to feel.

When the writer Adrienne Rich described motherhood as a channel for women's will to power, she landed on a truth about what people do when life has summarily crushed them. The child 'bullied and bribed into taking "one more bite" of a detested food', she wrote, is simply the sole available plaything of 'a woman restricted from acting on anything else except inert materials like dust and food'. In other words, the closer feeding comes to the burden of mothers alone, the closer motherhood comes to a kind of tyranny, however nested it may be in love. The mother, writes Rich, is 'both a numinous figure and the incarnation of evil', a veritable 'hoard of ambivalences'.

If every motherhood is a hoard of ambivalences where malice and care are mixed, it seems that we prefer to split our mothers, for ease, into heroines and villains. They are either Snow White cooking unbidden stew for her seven elderly 'children', or the psychopathic queen poisoning apples as she cackles at the thought of her stepdaughter buried alive. We scurry to root out the bad ones with their macrobiotic spells and unpredictable notions of freedom.

By some accounts – most famously that of feminist scholar Silvia Federici – the figure of the witch as we know her from medieval and early modern woman-hunting was born, in part, from panic over food. The early privatisation of land, Federici observes, replaced patterns of reliable self-sustenance with the spikes and crashes of commerce. Famine became a chronic feature of sixteenth-century life right when women's role (as keepers of the home) was cleaved apart from that of wage-earning men. Galloping malnutrition coincided, then, with the trial and execution of endless witches. Blamed for everyone's hunger, the witch became the repository for a hatred that should have been channelled elsewhere.

Historian Diane Purkiss has catalogued the ways in which early modern stories of witchcraft focus obsessively on food. All over these stories, women are poisoning and cursing apples, cakes and bread whose recipients sicken on contact. Sometimes all it seemed to take was the mention of food, or its mere handing over, to fill the victim's guts with illness, turn their breastmilk bad or send them into frothing convulsions.

The pressure was on for women, and mothers most of all, to protect the bounds of their households. Women, Purkiss explains, were meant to be tamers of nature, turning its fruits into something safe to eat. In their kitchens they would wash and boil what was dirty and uncooked and transform it into clean and palatable sustenance. Ideally, they'd manage to keep the ambient pestilence out of their homes. Those who failed to police the bounds of purity and pollution did violence to their status as women. The witch was an antihousewife who struggled or refused to make things behave as they should. Milk began to act like egg whites, vegetables rotted at speed, ale turned stinking and sour.

The pressures of stewarding everyone's nutrition in all but impossible times filled up women's bodies: the hands with which they cooked and cursed, the boobs from which they fed and the throats down which they themselves swallowed. Not only were women required to keep their own and their children's bodies free from the offerings of the devil, so too were they required to nourish themselves in a socially appropriate way. Purkiss recounts the trial for witchcraft of one Joan Jurdie, accused of causing the death of new mother Janet Murfin. It was apparently an early modern custom for childbirth to involve the gathering of local women, who'd ritually eat and drink with the woman stuck in bed. Joan had been invited, but failed to show up until after the baby's delivery, missing the occasion for performatively eating with the girls. Janet, in the wake of this insult, found *herself* unable to eat and helpless to feed her child. Janet, claimed the deponent, couldn't eat at all because Joan belligerently wouldn't. Witch begets witch, goes the story – one more woman goes weird about food, the milk from her nipples turned to blood.

Women can be witchfinders general in the rush to defend themselves, defining their own wholesome womanhood by calling out malevolent sisters. A long, unhappy lineage trails behind women's alertness to how other women eat; behind their unconcealed contempt for those whose appetites don't make sense. In di Prima's 'What I Ate Where', a long prose poem at the opening of her collection *Dinners and Nightmares*, the poet captures mercilessly the venom that can pass between women over dietary matters. The narrator describes a Thanksgiving feast for 1955: clams on the half shell, duck and filet mignon; white wine, pink wine, Italian sweets. Among the guests – Dan, Bill, Michael and Peter, is Dick, who 'whimsically married a bitch'. Dick eats everything, though tentatively. Millicent, the bitch, does not. She 'won't eat clams, or duck, or asparagus, or mushrooms. Nibbles at the pastry'. Millicent, we sense, is the wrong kind of woman. She wants an air conditioner in her forty-a-month East Side apartment, but more to the point, 'hates children and wants none. Had a successful miscarriage and several tantrums in hospital while recovering from it'. Those who 'invented' the feast, says our narrator, are bugged at Millicent's behaviour. But then again, 'this is how it would be when a woman comes to dinner in another woman's house'.

By contrast, in her career as a voice of feminist solidarity, di Prima's primary sympathies tended to err on the side of the witch. Repeatedly, she ascribed her own radicalisation to an era of 'endless witch-hunts', the McCarthyite condemnation of Communists like Ethel Rosenberg, fried in the electric chair for 'conspiracy to commit espionage' for the Soviets. Fried like no other woman in the States for nearly a hundred years. It might have made sense for then-President Eisenhower to commute Rosenberg's extraordinary sentence, but to do so, he feared, would inspire the Soviets to start recruiting other housewives too.

Though it was Julius, Ethel's husband, who had worked for defence contractors, and had all the access to secret information about new technologies – there was something equally suspicious, for the judge who tried them both, in a 'mature woman, almost three years older than her husband and almost seven years older than her brother'. A blight on feminine convention, Ethel was ruled to be of a piece with her spouse: not only a spy, whose crimes were judged 'worse than murder', but a kind of malevolent anti-parent. Though Ethel was obsessed, according to biographers, with perfecting modern mothering advice, the judge declared that it was 'love for their cause' that 'dominated [the Rosenberg's] lives'. A love, as he disdainfully put it, that was 'even greater than their love for their children'.

Di Prima was chilled by the ideological work that could be wrought in the name of defending good American motherhood. Yet, like Rosenberg, di Prima did not choose to fight the witch-hunt with actual witchcraft. She would unlikely have bothered to poison any cop, nor to tyrannise her children on purpose. Both were drawn to experiment with novel forms of parenting, like feeding on demand instead of rigidly synchronising children with the clock. Rosenberg came to these methods via the dicta of Dr Dorothy Whipple, who preached that babies should set their own agendas. Di Prima was reacting against her own mother's preference for scheduled care: 'ten minutes of nursing on each breast; burp 'em and put them back down in the crib. Never go in if they cry, never linger over the feeding. Pick them up again in four hours exactly.'

Yet while di Prima showed no witch-like interest in violating 'the house' – that airtight family unit – nor was she striving to make of herself a model of modern motherhood. Her aims were neither normative nor destructive of norms. Instead, they were radically creative, concerned with redefining the very concept of family. In capitalism's ideal scenario, the family lives for itself so it can live for gross national product. Children become a kind of project – an investment to be tended only in the most efficient ways. Di Prima saw caring for infants, like caring for each other, as un-wrenchable from living itself, and worth making room for by reaching beyond the resources of the private household. This meant sharing labour, pooling resources, demanding that kinship be more than biological or legal.

In the eyes of the state, a family is measured in births and deaths, but for di Prima we are each born 'a million times a day'. 'Each breath life and death', she writes: 'get up, put on your shoes, get / started, someone will finish' ('Revolutionary Letter #2'). Di Prima's experience of having been mothered in such a businesslike fashion gave her the sense that the Order of the World was at odds with human need. It was a realisation that came into almost unbearable focus with her first ever dose of peyote. 'I wept', she wrote of this discovery, 'for the soft and vulnerable flesh things of the world in a universe that seemed metal and precise as clockwork.' Her goal, after this, was to live, and to advocate for living, in a state of constant responsiveness to other people's flesh.

In Wales, my companions and I seemed quite determined to regulate our bodies like clocks. Bound as we were to the rest of the world, with its working and opening hours, its cycles of caffeination and anaesthetised sleep, most of us interpreted our teacher's invocations of 'harmony' and 'balance' in terms of our relation to these things. Sadie was particularly concerned to share her knowledge of breathing 'protocols' that helped to balance her alertness with her 'non-sleep resting' practice. Molly was anxious to harmonise her daily yoga schedule with her youngest child's shitting routine.

The mother from the past was to some extent prepared to humour us in these aims, advising her disciples on morning routines that could frontload daily enlightenment. On Day One she schooled us, for example, in.the virtues of the 'intermittent fast'. It was best, she advised, to limit eating time to an eight-hour window each day. For her, this meant a diet of nothing before noon and more nothing after 8 p.m. Since the mother from the past did not elaborate on what was 'best' about this, and since the group had surrendered our phones, we largely took this on faith for the remainder of the week.

Mostly, though, the retreat was supposed to *remove* us from the world of senseless body hacking and calendar alerts. As we gathered in a circle each morning, afternoon and night to breathe, blast out mantras, feel gongs, the mother from the past prepared us to abandon all judgement, exit the plane of thought. No longer would we bother ourselves with one another's earthly opinions, count the wrinkles round each other's mouths. We were going to enter the sphere of pure collective presence, melt into a soup of together.

For days I worried extravagantly that 'exiting the plane of thought' might precipitate thoughts I wouldn't be proud of. A damp, Christmas-movie epiphany, for instance, of everyone being 'the same'. This would be the start of my adult descent into blissed-out liberal complacency, drawing me ever downwards to the inevitable conclusion that it's really no big deal if ageing landlords want to parasitise the young for an easy life. 'Everything would be fine,' I saw my dumb future self pontificating at weddings, 'if all of us just sat down and took some deep breaths.'

The thought, if it came, turned out to be an inferior match for the gong, which drowned me out with its thunder. I struggle now to imagine even the cleverest of suspicions surviving that juddering metal. Each night, we took a big group bath in a noise so deep and grave that it felt like a warning – a scholastic reminder of the smallness of our plans and the greatness in surrendering them to fate. I wondered if this was some kind of modicum of what the spiritually or psychoanalytically inclined would have called the 'oceanic' – the feeling of total oneness with the world outside the jelly of our so-called bodies. Shunted off the escalator of ordinary time, we had fallen into a sea of everything, and everything included one another.

The feeling only got deeper, more alarmingly true, as we chanted in cacophonous unison, our wobbling voices amplified to more than the sum of their volumes. Deeper still as we spent what felt like forever observing the passage of air through our nostrils. Out of yours and into mine, exhaled, inhaled, exhaled, sucking up your yin and sending out my yang. With time (though who can say how much?) I began to feel the extent to which my hardened inner life shared space with fresher things: air, ideas and people I had most of my life been breathing in unnoticed. I sensed, with a kind of sad humour, that no matter how little I ate, these things would find their own sweet way into my lungs, and from there into the current of my bloodstream. We might not all live as equals, I thought, or be interested in socialist values. But what if this doesn't stop us being made of one another?

What, then, to do with our ambivalent 'interconnection'; how to reclaim it from over-sweetened talk?

Di Prima, no smug liberal, agreed that we were 'endless as the sea, not separable' ('Revolutionary Letter #2'). This was a shock to her too. It was a shock that came not just through meditation, but also more obscurely through the European literature of alchemy. In 1965, di Prima was invited to write an introduction to an edition of the work of Paracelsus, the fourteenth- and fifteenth-century Swiss physician, philosopher and alchemist. She wouldn't have guessed that a man like this would change her view of the world, but found on first reading that even his most baffling sentences sounded true.

She wasn't even clear, at this point, what exactly 'alchemy' meant, but its language gave her a feeling of instant recognition: that feeling 'when one's whole being says "yes" to a painting, a piece of music, even though it is like nothing we've known before, even though it takes an incredible stretch to stay with it'.

When she did write an informed appreciation of Paracelsus's work, di Prima focused her understanding of alchemy on his notion of a *materia prima* – a single substance or principle from which everything is built. 'How unlike our concept of the elements,' she marvelled, our method of cataloguing difference, 'separate and distinguishable, static and unchanging!' In alchemy, the one, original kind of matter can grow and mutate and shift, its offshoots recombining to create an infinity of new possibilities. This matter was the 'increatum', the not-yet-created, 'the one unique mother of all mortal things'.

Was everyone, according to this logic, a mother to everyone else? 'You will grow / a thousand times in the bellies of your sisters,' di Prima insisted. You will be midwifed, however reluctantly, by other people's proximate existence. Alchemy seemed to describe a kind of meeting of basic 'stuff' with boundless creativity, a promise of humans' capacity, if we used our imaginations, to make entire new worlds with whatever was to hand.

'[W]hat right have you got to breathe out just because you breathed in[?]' says an Old Family Friend to the narrator of *Dinners and Nightmares*. They are eating Chinese food and the young narrator's pregnancy is being accused of 'killing' her parents. He continues: '[A]nd there are already too many babies in ny [New York].'

Di Prima made worlds to accommodate her right and desire to breathe out; to make as many children as she wanted and could without the suffering society had designed for her. In order to do this, she presumably had had to subscribe to a certain meaning of interdependence: not that we are all the same, but that nothing, neither a person nor the world itself, can be changed in isolation. To soften the hostile position of a Family Friend who is also, in effect, your class enemy, you must act to change nothing less than the texture of class relations themselves. To change nothing less than the texture of class relations themselves, you must somehow feed the belief in, or desire for, such change in individual people.

That taste of easy abundance di Prima first experienced in California – plums and figs and flowing wine and children cared for in common – was in fact her inspiration to have a second child. There, she felt it was possible 'to live without struggle, or to have a different relationship with struggle'. Unlike those who believed that there were too many people for the earth's supply of food, she knew that it was possible, collectively, to alchemise better times.

Of course, it is always possible, when cooking, to alchemise something toxic – a hag's narcotic apple; a banquet for the cops. Riffing on Paracelsus's scheme of three key types of matter – mercury, sulphur and salt – di Prima's 'Revolutionary Letter #54' points to the havoc you can wreak with a seemingly neutral substance; when mercury gets in your food and sulphur in the air, and you are eating in a cloud of warfare. Get them with plenty of macrobiotic salt, di Prima sarcastically enjoins, and cook in the heat of an atomic explosion. As with macrobiotics (at least if generously construed), the principles of eating matter as much as the food itself.

What use is it to choose the 'right' goods in a world where all that is good has been poisoned?

I resolved not to poison my companions. I decided to see instead if anything good could be alchemised between us. To see what could be done with our incrementally mounting awareness of each other. I would try to listen out for their desires, and would try to respond in how I cooked. I would try to find a way, within this meeting of their needs, to hear and articulate my own.

Despite our teacher's talent for persuading us to practise *discipline* with movement and breath – her elegance in having us submit, for example, to the ordeal of kundalini yoga – most of us could not be persuaded to do this on an empty stomach. Despite our assurance that fasting was a very good thing, most of us were hungry on waking, and inclined to address that hunger with food. I let it be known in a whisper, which travelled at speed, that I'd be down in the kitchen each morning, just in case anyone else felt like being there too. One tentative pan of porridge very quickly became a vat, and as the guilt began to drain from my companions' morning meals, their tastes became more forthcoming. The vat got creamier, sugary, sprinkled with toasted, salted nuts. Some of the bowls were scattered with fat autumn fruits, slicked with syrup and globs of nut butter.

I did not join my companions in embellishing my porridge. In this, I knew, I was exposing myself to all the suspicions that descend on cooks who don't eat. Yet I got no sense that those around me cared that much about my non-participation. Why should they? This was not a competition of wills, but a meeting of basic desires.

Cooking will always involve a degree of controlling others – the cook must make certain choices on behalf of those they are feeding. Sometimes they will make these choices *in spite of* the eater's desires – misshaping every detail of the what, the how, and how much another person eats. Yet sometimes the cook is merely choosing how to interpret the eater's requests, how to translate their desire into a meal.

Hearing, sensing, guessing or feeling the eater's appetites is always an available option – to guide a meal, rather than dictating it. Perhaps it is more this distinction, rather than the cook's own appetite, that determines the difference between motherly care and maternal control in the kitchen. I had no more interest in fattening my companions to control them than I did in fattening them for the chop. Mostly, I just cooked porridge and handed it around.

Was this taking a cop to breakfast? Perhaps, but not with a view to feeding anyone's cop-hood. It would be nice to think that, instead, I was feeding their assumption that hunger is worthy of attention. Quite anti-cop, in fact, to attend to people's needs, to affirm the right to eat well. The fruit, then, was neither an endorsement of the cops nor a calorific Trojan horse. It was simply a gesture towards a particular way of being – a taste of shared respect for the 'soft and vulnerable flesh'.

Di Prima herself claimed to experience new potential as a taste. When, aged fourteen, she first discovered Romantic poetry, its 'tone of passionate urgency', something, as she puts it, stirred in her like kundalini – the serpentine yogic energy coiled at the base of the spine. Something filled her belly and rose to her throat: 'the taste of possibility'.

Di Prima never claimed that poetry could reconstruct the world, at least not from beginning to end. In her inaugural address as Poet Laureate for San Francisco in 2009, she described the New York she had grown up in – the New York of the 1950s – as a place where 'one wrote one's dreams, but didn't try to make them happen'. Still, it was poems she shouted from the steps of City Hall when, a decade later, she came to California for the 'grace of possibility' that had opened on that coast. You can neither write nor eat an idea into realisation, but the process begins with a verse, a sensation, a taste.

If inspiration could feel like eating, eating like inspiration, what kind of cooking would it take to bring this magic about? 'Do not try to control the breath,' said the mother from the past. 'Just observe what it does when you allow it.'

I tried to observe what happened when I cooked like someone who cared. Cared what it tasted like; cared what it would do. At that time, though I'd still been intent on making my meals taste good, cooking for myself was always chiefly governed by a principle of bearable minimalism. What were the fewest, cheapest ingredients at hand to stall my perpetual hunger – the lightest load of cultural and intellectual baggage? You do not need oil to toast a walnut. You do not need to have walnuts at all. All you need is hot carbohydrates, something salty to help them down. Now I was tossing chopped walnuts in a puddle of hot fat tall enough to make them toasty all the way through. You don't need oil to toast a walnut, but it makes the toasting more even, and leaves you with a bittersweet liquid to flavour the rest of your dish. I gathered in my hands more walnuts than I thought we could afford for the base of my aubergine stew. I caramelised some onions in the leftover grease, adding more until they exhaled. Thirsty onions hiss like they're sucking in air; it's better if they sound like they're spitting. I swirled a bottle of pomegranate syrup into the mix until big, hot bubbles bloomed. All of this made for a stew unfamiliarly rich, if hardly extravagant or weird.

This was pleasing, but it didn't stop the aubergines from softening too quickly, or quicker than I meant for them to do. I wanted them to keep their pillowy heft while slowly absorbing the smells and flavours in the rest of the pot. Instead, they sort of melted into a dark, sticky sea to wallow in until the rest was ready. Until there was also salad, people and steamed white rice to give the aubergine purpose.

Caring could improve, but never guarantee, the effect of my cooking endeavours. There was always a kind of dance between the vegetables and myself, between my own sense of time and the rhythms of heat-accumulation in heavy-bottomed pans. There was the pressure of my hands and my intentions, and the weightless process itself. Whatever I sank in, something else floated out; wherever there was yang, there was yin.

The force of yang can be understood as a kind of constriction – an application of weight, a move towards the centre, a grounding in the earth. Yet if eating is in some sense yang – a swallowing down, a centripetal action – feeding might instead be experienced as yin, a centrifugal release. Release gives way to more constriction; constriction to release. If then, potatoes are essentially yin, even the yinnest of all vegetables, perhaps this isn't all they can be. My handling of ingredients felt like an act of preparation that could never fully predict the capricious process of cooking.

A potato is one thing when you pull it out the ground, scrub and peel it into submission. Roast it, however, and you'll likely find you have alchemised something else. Much of its weight will have been lost as steam and condensed on the oven door. Its wet, oily face may have suntanned into a scraggly crust or shrivelled into a bitter second skin. It is now a potential object of pleasure or disgust, an object of imminent use. It is now a public potato; its taste may have been your design, but its promises are out of your hands.

For the Diggers, feeding people was an act of 'living theatre', a kind of imaginative performance. In a world where the idea of a 'free store' was almost incomprehensible – a store being typically the place where you went to spend your money – it took a certain amount of publicly doing fanciful things to get the point across. The way to show that people could grow, make, steal and barter for things on each other's behalf was to play this all out in public space. 'The way to be a cook is to cook,' wrote the California-Buddhist authors of *Tassajara Cooking*. Countercultural cafés, happenings and stores were places of improvisation – imagine the thing, try to do it and see what magic comes out.

There was no war, di Prima thought, that could not ultimately be traced to the war on the imagination. The imagination's starvation was the ultimate famine; the response was to keep seeking new worlds. That which you had been given, for di Prima, was not enough to sustain a good life. That which you imagined was instead 'a living weapon in yr hand'.

It seems likely, given the evidence, that Digger food was actually quite shit. Leaflets advertised 'good hot stew', 'ripe tomatoes', 'fresh fruit', but historian Charles Perry points to the patchy availability of decent quality leftovers. The meat was mostly unsaleable trimmings – turkey necks, chicken wings. Vegetables tended to be limp by the time they were procured, which affected the calibre of the stew. Bread, which came from two bakeries, was always one day old. Nevertheless, when di Prima drove this stuff to happenings and communes, she aspired to 'festive communal banquets' and 'elegantly served' home deliveries. She'd dreamt, when she arrived, of a particular San Francisco, and would keep trying to dream it into being. As she described it in her 2009 address, that city was a place 'where no one is hungry . . . where everyone shares their music, their food, their vision with everyone else'. It was a place where the alchemical magic of food was continuous with the magic of art – not a glue for disparate people, casting an illusion of vacuous sameness, but an engine for transforming their experience of life.

This dreamt-of San Francisco was a place of what Sophie Lewis would call 'mothering against motherhood', where people take care of children, regardless of biological ties, where young people educate and entertain kids, amuse and learn from the old. *'What happened folks?'* di Prima finally asks in her address. Maybe folks stopped believing in magic.

What a shame, since the Diggers' living theatre had proved that fantasies could flourish. Even if this was only true, in their case, on a miniature scale. Just as a cook can only ever work with what they have, put it in front of hungry people and watch for the result, the Diggers were the kind of activists who simply made proposals and saw how they worked among their group. 'Proposition not opposition,' they wrote in a speech published in 1968, 'proposals for a new

society, based on a new consciousness . . . [put] into operation on a small scale, mutually, into operation as an *example*.'
Utopia, for the Diggers, was yet to be defined, worked out
through experiments in living. The vision came from com-
munist ideology; the method from Zen spontaneity.

At times, these experiments left much to be desired, particularly for Digger women. Despite the fact, as Federici
observes, that it was women who lost out the most from
the sixteenth- and seventeenth-century land enclosures,
and women who continued to suffer the resulting gendered
hierarchy of labour, the twentieth-century Diggers never
managed to expunge this dynamic from their own organisation. Who was to open up the free restaurants but the
gang's 'old ladies'? Who was obliged to cook while their
'brothers' chose to hunt and gather food and give speeches
instead? Digger women complained of 'puttering over all
that brown rice while the guys go off to create the new
world'. Di Prima's positive experience of communal domes-
ticity notwithstanding, on some Digger farms it was women
alone who were yoked to cycles of cooking, cleaning, baking,
feeding children, feeding chickens and feeding indolent men.

Which is not to say that modern Digger operations
owed nothing to feminist precedent. Federici narrates the
history of seventeenth-century food riots as mostly woman-
engineered. 'Ruined', as she puts it, by price hikes and their
consignment to unwaged work, women were dependent
not just on cheap food, but on men for their access to it.
Systematic ruin was their spur onto the streets, where they
brandished their children's corpses, stormed bakeries where
grain was being embezzled, and rioted in market squares.
They ambushed carts of corn with pitchforks and sticks, and

poached and stole from rich neighbours' homes. The California Diggers' propensity, then, to seize what was 'theirs' had obvious feminist forebears, however underdeveloped their day-to-day feminist praxis.

Like the movement that first inspired them, the Diggers' ambition was never to realise a full-blown utopia, but rather to experiment with its ingredients. The original Diggers had been a seventeenth-century English agrarian group, who emerged in response to the devastating effects of land privatisation. The enclosure of land that had once been common, they thought, had made those who weren't 'teachers and rulers' into 'Servants and Slaves'. 'Take note', they declared in 1649, when they started cultivating land on St George's Hill in Surrey, 'that England is not a Free People till the Poor that have no Land have a free allowance to dig and labour the Commons, and so live as Comfortably as the Landlords that live in their Inclosures.' While their spiritual objection was at bottom to the ownership of space, their immediate ambition was not to overhaul property law; it was merely, as befit their resources, to carve out something decent for the poor in the margins of a spoken-for landscape. The California Diggers, in this vein, never yelled about 'dismantling' the capitalist state, however ridiculous the money system may have seemed to them as a means of distributing resources.

Movements, much like everything, are born from each other's ghosts, and never, it would seem, fully grown. And though we might rightly judge the California Diggers for their disappointing gender politics, it is harder to object to the modest scale or experimental manner of their work. This, to their minds, was both fitting and strategic – a means of proposing something of what a revolution might look like without having to wait for revolution. Like their English predecessors, the California Diggers believed in the value of making something good from within a bad situation. Rather than lumbering themselves – a mere glorified theatre troupe – with the burden of global working-class revolution, the Diggers thought it best to 'first free the space, goods and services. Let the theories of economics follow social facts.'

This freeing of goods and services was more than a mere redistribution of food as property. In fact, the 'Free Families' like the Diggers tried to imagine social relations ungrounded in such sordid things as ownership. The Diggers' network of communes was far from a retreat of righteous friends to their holes outside of society; rather it was an attempt to grow a social mode from the seed of communal activity. This effort extended to all the essential infrastructures of living. In 'Revolutionary Letter #15', di Prima instructed those who would seize a town to seize the power stations, water, transportation. Take what you need, she concluded; *it's free because it's yours*.

The 'summer of love' the Diggers tried to feed in 1967 famously turned cold. The 'grace of possibility' di Prima had seen remained a possibility alone. Yet however we understand the withering of the countercultural project, its notion of food as a basic right can never now be purged. The Diggers themselves believed it was a stretch to simply ask their old ladies to cook up utopia, to bundle their aprons and spoons in a van and bake a pie in the sky. The point, however, was to 'get up, put on your shoes, get / started, someone will finish'. 'NO ONE WAY WORKS', di Prima screamed in

'Revolutionary Letter #8', 'it will take all of us / shoving at the thing from all sides / to bring it down'.

As the mother and I loaded leftover cake and potatoes into the car, I wondered whether, when we returned from this retreat, I might truly return from my own. Whether I might find a place to cook that didn't just make 'something' possible, but something politically meaningful. To feed other people is not, in itself, a particularly radical act. Only rarely does it have to do with actual public service, or building a desire for living in common. Still, if you could subtly shift someone's sense of what was true about needs, about care, simply by feeding them a bowl of boiled oats on an expensive healing retreat, imagine what you could do with more purpose, more people – a 'living theatre' of comrades, not companions.

I did not yet have any idea what a more politicised feeding might look like, but wasn't that kind of detail one for the angels to reveal? As the mother from the past had convinced me, the leap was to believe that what you wanted was worth the danger of wanting. For that, you had to believe that what you wanted existed in the realm of possibility. Why not start with that, I persuaded myself, then work out how to feed it.

When I think of those retreaters – Milo and Sadie among them – who knew what they wanted from life, I remember them not just as caricatures of aspirant human capital, but also as exquisitely effortless eaters. Whether or not they shared di Prima's vision (they didn't), this they had in common with the poet. We are talking about a woman who made an entire book of catalogued meals: nine-hour

Thanksgiving dinners finished with pastries, panforte and fruit; 'beers and tears' and eels and Lipton's soup and for some reason many English muffins. Di Prima gives the impression of a woman who ate for the moment at hand: for the occasion, according to what she could find, in tune with the people around her.

If di Prima, unlike the enemy Millicent, was indeed an excellent eater, I doubt this was to prove any point – to prove herself a trustworthy feeder, worthy mother, good woman, non-bitch. Di Prima's desires – for a city where no one was hungry and everyone shared their food – were grounded in a widespread collective belief that such things were both reasonable and possible. Perhaps di Prima fed herself not because she believed that she should, but because she assumed that it was worth it. Not just because every brother should have what he needed to do his thing, but because she was invested in making it so.

The idea of feeding others with such purpose – of finding purpose in anything at all, acted on me in ways I could not have predicted. I left the retreat more assured than I had been in several years that I might, in fact, one day inhabit the body of a mother. My vision of this, however, did not start with childbearing hips and soft, rounded edges, no matter how much that vision of fertility had paraded itself as an ideal. Word on the street, other women and eating disorder treatment had all seemed to insist that a fertile body was an end in itself; that the dream of producing a child should motivate you to cultivate health, should irresist you to feminine fullness. But what was the point in all that if you had no faith in a social world worth reproducing into, not to mention if you had no interest in reproducing that way?

That faith in a better world, it seemed, would have to come first; my body, I found myself trusting, would bend and extend to its demands. It was not fertility, per se, but that *optimism of the will* that would allow me to sustain another life, whether or not I would ever create and gestate such a thing within my own body. It was only that faith, in the end, and not some feminine or familial ideal, that could inspire me to inspire a human child. To show a child what life is; to try and love it with them for the rest of my own existence.

As it happened, another heart did beat in my belly eighteen months later. I could not have imagined how I'd feed it until it was lodged, unmistakably, there. I had leapt into something that my body, lit with feral determination, would surely help to lead me through. For at least as long as it had taken to conceive the little thing, it seemed I had believed in the possibility of a world worth ejecting it into. Now, my body called me to do everything it could to grow the little bastard big. That creature alchemised in me a flamboyant desire for foods that had never interested me before – most of them salty, otherwise bland but bottomless, urgent and big.

The moment she decided to get pregnant, 'by herself' if not alone, di Prima wrote a 'Song for [her] Baby-O, Unborn': 'I won't promise / you'll never go hungry', she wrote, 'but I can show you . . . enough to love / to break your heart'. She did not doubt that the world was harsh or would subject a child to pain, but nor did she believe that this was all. She believed in the chance, decided to live for the chance, that this gutted, breaking globe could do better.

5

You Ask

I was not unused to the sensation that some sparkling future had suddenly been called off. With the defeat, in 2019, of a socialist Labour Party in the UK general election, concurrent with that of Bernie Sanders in the US Democratic primaries, a number of solid-looking plans had rarefied overnight into a vapour of insubstantial fantasies: the idea of accessible healthcare, a pre-death retirement age, minimum wages that could buy people food. It was now the apparent duty of the Left to admit that these ambitions had been absurd. In the days and weeks that followed, the defeated warned each other against the temptation to wallow. Against the trap of carrying an out-of-date dream inside us for ever. We scuttled back to pubs and meeting rooms to try to *make new plans*, but newness doesn't thrive on despair. We talked about 'getting more local', of a 'return to the grassroots', but it all seemed a little vague.

When 2020 unleashed a pandemic that concentrated governments' powers of resource maldistribution, the proportion of UK households without enough food rose from 9 per cent to over 15 per cent. At the same time, 15 per cent more people than before were diagnosed with eating disorders, struggling to feed ourselves despite the fact that many of us could afford to. We, that 15 per cent, began to eat, quite literally, like there was no tomorrow, whether that meant we ate a lot or almost nothing at all.

When four years later I was told that my unborn baby's heart had stopped beating, I harboured more literal thoughts of what it might mean to carry a cancelled future inside you. I carried something cancelled for four more days while I waited for its surgical extraction. Within those days, my swollen boobs shrank back to square one and my bottomless craving for one-note, salty food abruptly found its bottom. All that eating, it seemed, had failed to grow the little bastard bigger than a fig.

On the day of the surgery, I was once again instructed not to eat until late afternoon – the earliest conceivable time I'd be woken from chemical sleep. You'd think a bit of fasting wouldn't bother a person so supposedly preoccupied with loss and plummeting hormones. But while I waited for a procedure so grim it seemed it would be better not to give it too much thought, I worried I'd be judged for pulling out my phone or visibly reading a book. So instead, while I stared for several hours at the wall, I thought about what I'd have for dinner.

I thought of all the dinners I'd had in recent months – all the nourishment I'd hoped would manifest a child but ultimately hadn't. Piles of potatoes and chapatis and rice and toast and noodles and pasta and all the other things you're meant to eat with them if you want enough protein and fat. I thought about how I would eat them again, and then again, whether or not I would ever end up growing another life.

In her 2024 book *Burnout*, the political historian Hannah Proctor asks how it is possible to survive defeat without feeling as though the future has been cancelled. She is not talking about personal disappointments, but rather the kinds of defeat routinely faced by the political Left – the setbacks that inevitably come with an upwind struggle to transform the social world. Proctor's 'future' refers to a horizon of social justice – a future that for many represents the only future; the only thinkable alternative to mass immiseration and climate destruction.

To feel the impossibility of this future – the thing we all live towards – is very hard to survive. It is, I have come to believe, precisely the kind of thing that might make eating feel pointless, even obscene. The 'left melancholic', as defined by philosopher Walter Benjamin, is a creature half-mad with disappointment, so outraged by defeat as to position themselves, forever more, to the left of 'what is in general possible'. You might say that the anorexic, also stumped in the face of despair, does something similarly obtuse when she takes her own body to the threshold of survival. Latching onto an impossible task – to die without actually dying – she thrives on the sense of having a cause, despite its lack of promise or purpose. Perhaps this is a way of surviving the conviction that the causes that actually matter are doomed; that the only future worth living won't ever come to be. But this was not the future that, for seven long weeks, bled brightly into my pants.

The idea of growing a foetus until it bust into the world was certainly one future I had cherished, but never had it been the condition of my faith in a better world. Conceiving a child had not been the point of trying to develop new strength, new hope and new political will; just a particularly stunning result of these things. My commitment to life came first; the desire to have a child was its mere affirmation. A child might have anchored or even secured this commitment with their presence – externalised my need to keep believing that the world was ours to create – but it was that belief, and not the baby itself, that had made it possible to eat. Thanks for nothing, Eating Disorder Unit, I thought in my recovery cubicle as I munched on hospital digestives; thanks for nothing, fertility podcasts. I did it all without you.

How I had done this – by which I mean reached a point of being able to eat without despair or ennui – is in part the subject of what I am about to tell you. But it is also what you have already read. As I discovered in my search for a relief meal, much of the relief had already been felt, if only in strange and momentary snatches – in slices of Marinara pizza, uncounted dumplings, clandestine porridge. At times when the act of eating felt connected not to exploitation and corporate greed, but rather to solidarity with animals, working people and women; to the erotic imperative of making easy abundance for all; to the project of feeding new comrades and of living by the idea that everyone should have what they needed to do their thing. Though unexamined as such at the time, these moments of eating lived on in my body as pieces of evidence – clues as to what it might take to eat with confidence, without having to give it too much thought.

Perhaps the most substantial piece of evidence had surfaced two weeks after I came back to London from Wales; still several months before my conscious search for a 'relief meal' began. I am speaking of a meal that took the form of some overcooked grains, piled high on a paper plate. Draped across them were some viscous vegetables, some of them livid, some of them beige. They had been slid unceremoniously towards me across a trestle table in Parliament Square, where I'd walked, or more accurately 'marched' with hundreds of other people at a Landworkers' Alliance demonstration. In October 2022, the UK government was threatening changes to its environmental land management scheme, which subsidised farmers. International trade deals and policies grounded in market 'growth' were being mooted at the expense of livelihoods and access to affordable food. Farmers, as a result, along with food system workers and organisers in the environment, land and food justice movements, gathered to demand a food system grounded in need, and the universal right to food.

Like most things happening at that time which required any minimal investment of energy, I hadn't really wanted to go, but there I was anyway, following a tractor that had been driven all the way to London from Pembrokeshire: four days' travel at fifteen miles per hour, steered by a 74-year-old man. Perhaps it was all those vibrations I'd caught from the sound of the gong, or perhaps just Matt's insistence I go with him. Sometimes, if you are alive, he said, you have to go outside.

There are certain cancelled futures that demand we do more than grieve, accept and survive. Some things require that we act in response; that we maintain our political aspirations. As various speakers at the demonstration highlighted, we lived in the fifth wealthiest nation in the world, where a quarter of households with children couldn't afford enough food. The dearth of subsidies for farmers was part of this – making the cost of staple foods even higher – but so were unfeasibly low wages and the dwindling value of benefits.

Energy costs were so high that food banks, where more and more people had to trek for the merest calories, reported that people were asking for food that didn't need a fridge or a cooker to store and cook it. That year, the Food Foundation had surveyed UK households about their ability to get enough to eat. The organisation was so shocked by the rate of food insecurity that it widened and reran the survey, only to get the same results.

While I ate my grains and vegetables in murky autumn sun, I listened to an organiser from the UK Right to Food campaign speak from a trailer lined with flowers and straw. In my own London borough, it seemed, there were people working with both local and national organisations to enshrine the right to decent food in policy and law. Hunger, the organiser barked, was not a sad fact of life but a brutal political choice. The campaign she represented called on government to respond to some basic-sounding demands: to ensure that all children in schools were given lunch for free, without the shame and social pressures of means testing; to account for the cost of food in minimum wages and benefits; to fund and organise community kitchens.

Food justice, the organiser argued, should be ensured in all varieties of policy: in competition law, planning, transport and all other matters of local governance. Instead of an emergency food system reliant on charities and private companies, subjecting people to postcode lotteries and humiliating referral systems, food should be procured and distributed at the level of local government, which should understand and respond to constituents' social and cultural needs. A community resourced on principles of justice, she said, of equality, dignity and love – would be a community with the means to eat together. Solidarity, not charity, was the animating principle behind this campaign.

In this, the Right to Food campaign drew, and continues to draw, inspiration from the Black Panther Party's survival programmes. The first of these, the Free Breakfast for School Children scheme, was started in Oakland, California in 1969, and quickly spread to party chapters across the USA. One of its founders, Elaine Brown, had been inspired as a student at UCLA to requisition the oodles of college food that ended up in the garbage each day, persuading dormitory officials to 'dump the leftover food on the party' instead.

The Panthers used this kind of ingenuity to gather enough eggs, bacon, sausage and grits to feed 15–30,000 hungry children each day. Volunteer labour, food donations and financial contributions from local businesses produced enough to set a standard of what a decent morning meal should look like. Under the guidance of Bobby Seale, the programme expanded to include what Brown describes as 'the most magnificent food giveaways . . . major community events'. What had started as breakfast for children blossomed into bags of groceries for whole families, a stalking panther printed on each one.

To call this charity would miss the programme's strategic role as a public performance and a site of political education. By demonstrating the extent of basic necessities denied by the state to Black children, the Panthers poured shame on California, and the US government more broadly. According to poet and one-time Panther Judy Juanita, the aim was 'to show the community and the government "This is what a just society should do." In a just society, particularly one that is as wealthy as this one, no children should be going to school hungry.' In 1975, the state would adopt its own free breakfast programme – the first of many federally funded initiatives that persist to this day.

But crucially, the programme showed Black children what they should expect and demand of the state – as Lorde would put it, that 'internal sense of satisfaction to which, once we have experienced it, we know we can aspire'. Framing hunger as the evidence of oppression, the Panthers drew a line between unequal access to food and the racialised dynamics of capitalism. Alongside their free breakfasts, they set up 'liberation schools', where children and adults studied the ideas of Frantz Fanon and Malcolm X, Karl Marx and Che Guevara. The food helped children concentrate better on these things, but it also gave form, in their mouths and in their bellies, to the truth of their right to food. Food and education as well as health care, housing and employment – other targets of the Panther's survival programmes. 'Survival pending revolution' was the aim – no point in one without the hope of the other.

The Black Panthers' Free Breakfast Programme, then, supplied not just food but a new generation of radicals. As Brown put it, 'The more the party sharpened the contradictions between haves and have-nots, between the powerful and the powerless, the oppressor and the oppressed, the more the people would seek to resolve them.' Food was not just a thing to be sought, it was fuel for the act of seeking – a fuel for the act of growing a political consciousness. 'Your body belongs to the revolution,' said Norma Armour Mtume, who ran medical clinics for the party, 'so you have to take care of it.'

Just as the modern Right to Food movement has grown around the struggles of farmworkers and other food justice organisations, the Black Panthers' survival programmes developed in tandem with those of the Diggers and the United Farm Workers (UFW) union. Reflecting on her early education in the Panther doctrine, Juanita recalls the Experimental College set up within San Francisco State University, which aimed to further the cause of Black Studies. On lawns, in cafeterias and other semi-public spaces, representatives from the Diggers would teach ad-hoc classes about their own free food programmes. Brown reports that at Black student meetings in UCLA, comrades began to foreswear their accustomed Gallo wine when the United Farm Workers called for a boycott of their grapes.

The struggle for farmworkers' rights fed in turn on the principles of Black power – the idea, for example, that rather than accepting recourse to charity, those who lost out to the capitalist system should build momentum within their ranks. This was one of the central aims of the 1960s grape strike, where growers in California protested cuts to their wages at the height of harvest season. Led by Chicanx civil rights activists César Chávez and Dolores Huerta, the UFW organised the strike in combination with a mass consumer boycott – a means to use economic pressure to advance negotiations with growers and bring about legislative protections for workers.

Chávez and Huerta were themselves inspired by the non-violent tactics of Gandhi and Martin Luther King, and were moved, like the Panthers, by the evident undernourishment of farmworkers' children. Huerta, as a schoolteacher in the 1950s, had seen the extent of child hunger and reasoned that one of the best ways to feed hungry children would be to organise the farmers and farmworkers who fed them. The

strikes and boycotts were hard on those farmers, demanding they picket and go without pay in the service of their
future freedom. As well as targeting economic mechanisms,
the boycott called on everyone to stand in solidarity with
these sacrifices.

While President Reagan performatively snacked on
grapes, Dolores Huerta told the public: 'You have a responsibility to farmworkers because farmworkers feed you.' Her
instructions were clear. 'Fast!' she commanded. 'Don't eat
lettuce. Don't eat grapes. Don't drink wine. That's a very
simple thing for people to do.' She asked them to picket – a
more challenging demand unless you consider that 'a farmworker has to walk thousands of miles in his lifetime to
feed you'.

'Hunger is a political choice,' repeated the Right to
Food organiser, and all it would take to undo it were
equally straightforward choices. As I listened, this kind of
sentiment – the notion that change was not just a reasonable thing to want, but an imperative if you knew how to
make it – cut right through the nauseating discourse that
leftists had been served since 2019, the sneering of comfortable centrists, whose distaste for a potential socialist government
had been vindicated, they felt, by its annihilation at the ballot
box. These people, we were told, were realistic; their indifference to others' hunger was grown up. Their personal right
to food, they believed, was not owed to them by default,
but had been won through enlightened choices. If they ate
well, it was because they had worked hard for the flakiest
salt, the most virgin olive oil. If they ate meat, the meat was
admirably expensive – savoured in virtuous moderation. If
they were charitable, donating odd tins of beans from their

groaning weekly shops, they should be lauded for their mercy; those who had failed so abjectly to feed themselves should be grateful for these gifts.

The food I ate while I watched the Right to Food speech paid no heed to the aesthetics of virtue. It didn't brand itself as 'ethical' or 'plant-based' or a particularly health-conscious choice, but it was nourishing nonetheless, made without animal labour or flesh and without a gun to anyone's head.

This food had been provided by one of the many organisa-tions marching that day – La Via Campesina, the international movement of peasants, landless workers, indigenous people, rural women and migrant farmworkers. The organisation's primary mission is to defend peasant agriculture because doing so protects food sovereignty – people's right to healthy and culturally appropriate food. When people in any locality are able to define their own food and farming systems, the needs of those people, rather than those of corporations and markets, move to the centre of food distribution. For La Via Campesina, food sovereignty 'implies new social rela-tions free of oppression and inequality between men and women, peoples, racial groups, social and economic classes and generations'.

All this talk of meals, food traditions, food cultures as the product of collective decisions did something to how I saw that plate of grains. Food, it seemed, could be more than a mere occasion for self-definition – self-aggrandisement, self-judgement, or performative self-defence. To accept this food was not to have made a self-defining choice, but to embrace what a collective had been able to grow and cook and trans-port; what they had judged to be worthy fuel for a hungry, adult mob. The food did not encumber its eater with the baggage of class – with some measure of innocence or complicity in culinary violence – rather, it focused a crowd on what we were jointly able to *do* – how our bodies might work together against that violence's very existence.

What relief in the transformation of a meal from *my lunch* to *everyone's experience*. *My lunch*, after all – that thing we like to log and evaluate and judge – is on inspection hardly 'mine' at all. Though we might think of ourselves as empowered to curate what we eat and therefore to define who we are, our choices are most often arrayed for us by a food system grounded in profit. Food is parcelled into cultural niches and targeted where it will sell – virtue for those who can afford it and comfort for those who can't. While we might cherish our culinary preferences as marks of enlightened taste, they are often little more, to return to Barthes, than expressions of inherited status.

You would think this meal would then constitute an epiphanic moment – the one where I felt empowered to relinquish my disease and dedicate myself to the cause. But though I was briefly able to re-envisage eating as a creative, collective act, and more than just a means of self-distinction, I could not yet see how the same might apply to a person with an eating *disorder*. Anorexic, to my mind, was still very much a thing I *was* – an unfortunate and distinguishing error of the self. I was, it seemed, constitutionally weird about food, which disqualified any interest in its politics. My job, as the specialists perceived it, was not to care about things beyond the treatment at hand; my prime vocation was meal plans, target weights. *Refeeding first.* The rest of life later.

It was only the following year, when a synthesised mushroom, among other things, encouraged me to think about this anew, that I began to perceive anorexia not as an exception to our politics of food, but rather as a window onto its logic – a symptom of the solipsist's philosophy that you are what you eat (or what you don't). It was only then that the counterproductive obsession, among treatment specialists, with personalised 'meal plans' – joyless variations on a template for optimal eating – no longer seemed like the preserve of the diseased, but rather the formalisation of an unhappy norm: to think of eating in terms of 'one's diet' – one's personal ledger of values and achievements, nutritional and moral.

And it was only after mining, retrospectively, those moments of relief I have described – those occasions when eating felt generative of something beyond myself – that I finally felt ready to turn my hand to something new; something beyond the mere avoidance of food, or investigating why I was avoiding it. Only then, months after the protest, did I find myself inclined to get over myself and give the Right to Food woman a call.

The organiser asked me no questions about who I thought I was – if I was unqualified, overprivileged or sick. To her, it was enough that I was moved by the things that moved her to make things happen. I began to join meetings with others who organised protests and lobbying campaigns. I began to help raise funds, design research into the meaning of a 'right to food' for people in my borough. After a period of melancholy, MANTRA and institutionalised self-doubt, it felt like I had something to do. However slow the progress, or provisional the goals, it felt like I had one more thing to eat for.

In October 2023, the group was given cause to expand from its local focus, prioritising food justice issues on the international stage. To the list of demands I have mentioned was added: that the government work to end the use of food and health as weapons of war; that it recognise that Israel employs starvation as a weapon of war.

A good diet isn't always enough to keep an unborn baby alive, but a bad one will surely cause it harm. By bad, I mean the kind of diet a person would never freely choose for themselves – the kind experienced by over a million women in occupied Gaza.

Within two months of 7 October 2023, the UN body that monitors food security began to warn of famine in the region, with a majority of the population facing food insecurity classed as 'catastrophic'. Within a few months, a quarter of pregnant women in Gaza were eating only one type of food and more than half eating only two. Children began to go without food for days at a time; their faces turned yellow and their gums tumesced as they resorted to drinking sandy, salty water. Their teeth were worn from silica as they tried to survive on grass. Their parents set to grinding animal feed into flour. The definition of bread devolved into something made, for instance, from a combination of rabbit, donkey and pigeon feed. As Israeli forces opened fire on Palestinians who tried to get flour from looted aid trucks, the rest began to attempt to survive on straw.

The political choice to starve the Palestinian people in aid of a settler colonial project has a decades-long history. After the Second Intifada, or uprising, against the Israeli occupation, between the years 2000 and 2005, the state of Israel laid waste to Gaza's farmland, pulling up trees and ensuring that residents could no longer produce food for themselves. Over three-quarters of the population had relied on humanitarian aid for food even before the escalation into catastrophic hunger, thanks to the Israeli blockade of the region in 2007. In 2012, legal action taken by Israeli human rights group Gisha forced the government to reveal documentation showing that since 2008, their officials had been calculating the minimum caloric intake required to keep the Gazan people from starving, ensuring that no more food entered the region than was necessary by these measures. According to the Red Lines Policy, Palestinians warranted 37 per cent fewer fruits and vegetables than Israelis, 19 per cent less meat and 43 per cent less dairy.

Since the conflict became genocidal, even the minimal food coming through has been systematically blocked by violence and absurdist bureaucracy. The Rafah crossing, where aid is technically allowed to enter, is not equipped for massive commercial vehicles, and trucks are inspected several times and subjected to bogus regulations before they can be permitted through. The little food that does make it over is near impossible to distribute over the rubble from constant bombing, via roads that no longer exist, using blacked-out channels of communication. The purchase of food from Israel itself is prohibited to aid organisations, who instead must buy it from Egypt in a fatally inefficient dance. Trucks are blocked, burned and pillaged by soldiers; the intended recipients of their contents are shot. Palestinians' bakeries are bombed, their fuel and electricity cut off.

Whatever commitment there is to securing the Palestinian right to food, whether through immediate aid or the longer-term campaign to end the occupation, any kind of engagement in this cause flouts the dogma that there is nothing to be done. Just as food inequality more generally is posed as an accident of immutable 'systems', the hunger of Palestinians is routinely mythologised as the side-effect of ancient, immutable conflict. Though Israeli defence minister Yoav Gallant explicitly announced on 9 October 2023 that the settler state would ensure there was 'no electricity, no food, no fuel' for the people of Gaza, their starvation continues to be passed off as a kind of natural disaster – a *humanitarian crisis*, a *casualty of war*, a *tragedy* of fate. As though there were things so hard to understand that to try and understand them would be hubris.

When in April 2024 global attention was turned on World Central Kitchen – the organisation responsible for more than half of non-governmental food aid deliveries to Palestinians, seven of whose aid workers were killed in action by IDF forces – Prime Minister Benjamin Netanyahu called the incident an accident, a botched effort to bring down a suspected terrorist. This, despite the fact that the group had been moving in a so-called deconflicted zone by prior agreement with the IDF. Despite the fact that their three-vehicle convoy carried the World Central Kitchen logo, and took a route marked specifically for the passage of aid. Despite the fact that after one drone strike tore through one of the vans, there followed another and then a third. 'Unfortunately,' said Netanyahu, 'there was a tragic case of our forces unintentionally hitting innocent people,' as with the hundreds of other aid workers killed before and since. Then-US president Joe Biden concurred that this was a 'tragedy'; that Israel, rather than targeting those who sought to keep civilians alive, simply hadn't 'done enough' to protect them.

You do not need to believe in these narratives to be demoralised by their power. In fact, it is in part the very ludicrousness of what we are expected to hear that threatens to make resistance feel pointless. Even, or perhaps especially, within the Arab world, the idea of a right to food that might extend to the people of Gaza struggles against an onslaught of demoralisation tactics. In January 2024, Egyptian president Abdel Fattah el-Sisi used the Gazans' abject hunger as an excuse to ask Egyptians to put up with their own starvation. Despite Egypt's own role in managing the Rafah border, Sisi held up the people of Gaza as a living example 'sent by God' of 'people on the border who we cannot even send subsistence food items to'.

It should perhaps be no surprise, given the country's history of putting down insurgent activity, that early mass mobilisations in solidarity with Gaza quickly waned in the Egyptian context. The 'collective paralysis' described, in an essay on the Arab political subject by Egyptian writer Nihal El Aasar, can only be understood in terms of the counter-revolutionary processes that undid the gains of Tahrir Square. Yet as El Aasar points out, this kind of inertia has roots much deeper than a single historical moment. The forced presence of Israel in the Arab region has long served processes of capital accumulation, making the repeated defeat of the Arab people – within and beyond Gaza – a condition of the US-led, post-Soviet imperialist order. The idea of Israel as a democratic body was never meant to be believed – only to render the term 'democracy' conveniently meaningless; only to let state violence rip with the approval and support of Western powers. The Arab world El Aasar describes, marked for well over a decade by 'counterrevolution, regional warfare, tens of thousands of Arabs killed, tens of thousands more detained, economic dependency, sanctions, Western intervention, and increasing autocracy and repression', represents a site of intentional efforts of mass depoliticisation – a cocktail of methods through which to avert any dream of a free Palestine, pan-Arabism, Arab socialism.

Within the remoteness of the Anglosphere there has remained a remarkable tendency to believe in the unbelievable. To draw solace from the daydream that famine is a simple fact of life. The idea that death in general has no connection with human intention or power is already an everyday delusion – a story through which we allow ourselves to bear what is hardest to bear. As Sigmund Freud wrote in 1920 in 'Beyond the Pleasure Principle', 'If we are to die ourselves, and first to lose in death those who are dearest to us, it is easier to submit to a remorseless law of nature . . . than to a chance that might have been escaped.' Though the idea that Gaza's forced starvation is a natural process would seem to test this delusion beyond what it can withstand, there have always been those who are prepared to indulge in unlikely consolations.

Like the fantasy, for instance, that prior to Operation Al-Aqsa Flood the wounds of settler colonialism might have been healed through the sharing of hummus. In September 2012, while Gisha was engaged in a legal battle to force the Israeli Ministry of Defence to reveal its 'Red Lines' document – the one that would make explicit the state's long-term policy of undernourishing Palestinians – Israeli chef Yotam Ottolenghi and his Palestinian co-author Sami Tamimi jointly published their cookbook *Jerusalem*. In its introduction, they imagined that food – in their opinion 'the only unifying force in this highly fractured place' – might 'eventually bring Jerusalemites together, if nothing else will'. If you couldn't beat what they vaguely referred to as 'four thousand years of intense political and religious wrangling', perhaps you could find a way to enjoy its products. For the authors of *Jerusalem*, the 'positive side' of the brutal occupation was 'some fantastic food and culinary creativity'. 'There is something about the heated, highly animated spirit of the city's residents', they wrote, 'that creates unparalleled delicious food.'

The comforting notion that food will *bring us together* has, in recent years, sold a number of anglophone cookbooks: *Soup for Syria*; *Ripe Figs*; *The Kitchen Without Borders*. Though these books provide a certain visibility to struggles in Syria, Turkey, Greece, Cyprus, Iran, Eritrea and Venezuela, directing funds to conflict zones and refugee organisations, to idealise food as a comfort, a leveller and a healer, while failing to acknowledge its use as a weapon, is to conscript the act of cooking to the narrative of conflict as natural, rather than political. As historian N. A. Mansour has argued, portraits of 'resilient' cooks, making bread amid scenes of abjection, are alluring precisely for their apolitical 'politics' – the way they 'suggest that the conflicts they chronicle are perpetual ways of life, crises without origins and without end. As if we might as well not worry about when or why or how.'

More troublingly, scenes of culinary harmony in war zones also find their place in overtly political media. As the famine unfolds in Palestine and people eat hay, the Israeli army regularly publishes what it calls 'recent' footage of busy markets and restaurants in the southern centres of Gaza. While Israeli restaurateur Michael Solomonov has repeatedly used his food outlets to platform support for Israel, he describes cooking as an opportunity to 'expose people to a side of Israel [which has] nothing to do with politics'. Israeli newspaper *Haaretz* published one article celebrating the Israeli army's culinary resourcefulness, featuring photographs of soldiers cooking happily in the abandoned kitchens of Gazan families. One looks over his shoulder beaming as he stands at a chopping board surrounded by goods – a pot of hummus, fresh vegetables, a bowl of lemons and limes. Captions suggest that food has become a 'place of sanity' for the troops, who show off their best 'bruschetta alla Gaza'.

How do you struggle against a violence that claims not to exist? Thwart the intentions of a force that claims to have none? Is it possible to look at the gaslit, gaslighting grin of an IDF soldier – benignly re-styled as a cook – and feel anything other than the utter futility of resistance? The meaninglessness of words?

You would think, perhaps, that it wasn't, unless you were paying attention to the resistance that already does take place. For the charge against the violence of Israel was never going to be led by English-language cookbooks; it is led by Palestinians in Palestine. It is true that within Gazan refugee camps, there are people feeding each other, finding ways to make the food that reaches them taste at least something like the food they'd want to eat. But this is not simply cooking as a healing end-in-itself. For many, it is not just survival, or making the best of a bad lot, but survival pending revolution. As Palestinian campaigner Omar Barghouti has put it, Palestinians may be forced to prioritise survival, but they also 'aspire to live in a more just world, with no ranking and suffering, no hierarchy of human worth, and where everyone's rights and human dignity are cherished and upheld'.

Perhaps this is what the food blogger Hamada Shaqoura means when he says that he dreams to have the opportunity to dream. Shaqoura's now-famous Instagram account broadcasts his efforts, together with local volunteers, community kitchens and organisations like Watermelon Relief, to cook and serve as much food as possible to others displaced in Gaza. There is something uncanny in the format. We find on Shaqoura's feed familiar reels of ingredients slashed from their packages, poured from vessels, sizzled in oil and served to eager mouths. But the vessels are gigantic, the ingredients are crap and the chef doesn't smile for the camera. There is dignity in the food Shaqoura cooks, to be sure – spaghetti with white sauce, corn and bell peppers; rice pudding cooked on an open fire – but there is always a subtext of necessity, an evident gap between the cook's ingenuity and how he would cook if he were free. Among the videos of chicken wings crisping and apples being candied are links to GoFundMe pages and reminders to every follower to 'keep boycotting'.

The difference between the cookbook author or publisher who emphasises food's transcendent power and the likes of Shaqoura, who also makes a public display of hunger and resourcefulness, is that one betrays what Freud described as a placid respect for reality; the other something verging on militant disgust. To mourn with respect for reality is to fold your pain into an acceptance of the way things are. Yet there is defiance, rather than any sign of contentment, in the way Shaqoura tosses globs of minced meat onto burning hotplates; in the way he makes the best of canned cheese, tries to make pizza out of tortillas. He seeks to highlight not just the respect that Palestinians have for themselves despite their treatment as human meat, but also how much there is to lament in this opposition. Rather than mourning of the 'proper', adaptive sort that obviates political action, here is a pained response to violence that refuses to live by its terms or towards the dark future it prescribes.

So it seems that acting in solidarity with Gaza must involve that we not only send food into the region, but also, as Shaqoura insists, 'keep boycotting'. This is why the UK Right to Food campaign, when it began to demand that the government 'work to end the use of food and health as weapons of war', also, more specifically, demanded that it back the Palestinian Civil Society movement for boycott, divestment and sanctions (BDS). BDS, which came into being in 2005, calls on people around the world not to consume the products of companies that invest in Israel's illegal settlements or power its deadly weapons. It calls on unions to pressure their pension funds to divest from these firms and for governments to consider who they contract with by the same criteria. Inspired by the methods of the South-African anti-apartheid struggle and US civil rights movement, it is a form of non-violent resistance that over the years has encompassed public diplomacy, strikes, marches, the building of new institutions and the making of literature and art. It is a form of resistance that has come to the forefront of Palestine solidarity because, as history has shown, it can work.

If it is difficult to see how foregoing McDonald's chips could ever make a difference to 'four thousand years of intense religious and political wrangling', it is useful to note that this protest of the restaurant chain's donation of thousands of meals to Israeli soldiers has already had a 'meaningful business impact', according to chief executive Chris Kempczinski. These kinds of business impacts, if significant enough, are a powerful source of pressure on governments. But for BDS to be truly effective, the impacts must be steady, wide-ranging and deep. It wasn't until major corporations deemed it more costly to stay in South Africa than to leave that they withdrew their investment and presence; it wasn't until the campaign was carried by a critical mass of outrage that it forced the South African government to end its apartheid policies. According to Barghouti, one of the founders of the movement, BDS is supported by tens of millions of people from labour and farmworker unions, and racial, social, gender and climate justice movements, yet even more commitment is needed to force the state of Israel's hand.

Campaigns like BDS efficiently undermine the rhetoric of *nothing to be done*; the idea of God's plan, of human conflicts too deep and elemental for political solutions. Of impersonal political 'structures' too diffuse to be undone via trifling consumer choices. BDS is not, in fact, a matter of mere consumer choice, it is rather a consumption-based movement – one grounded in winnable targets, in working, like the Diggers, with the materials at hand. It is organised, not haphazard; strategic, not merely wishful; institutional, not individual. There is nothing individualist or trifling in a campaign that asks 'people of conscience' to consume in a way that galvanises further collective action. To 'fast' from McDonald's chips so that others might one day be better fed. To eat instead in a way that makes sense of the chant that in our thousands, in our millions, we are all Palestinians.

This is not, then, a case of feasting or fasting simply to make ourselves feel better. Of studying Ottolenghi's happy

marriages of ingredients, or rogue self-starvation in 'solidarity' with those who have no choice but to starve. There
are, it turns out, political ways to enjoy yourself and then
there is simply enjoyment. There are, it turns out, political ways to fast, and then there is gestural martyrdom.
When Simone Weil claimed to be starving in sympathy
with hungry soldiers in France, she had no reason to believe
that this 'protest' would result in any change of conditions.
Her love of suffering spoke to a rejection of the world; a
faith only in the promised life to come. When Palestinian prisoners go on hunger strike, they stand publicly as a
measure of Israel's disregard for due process. They show a
willingness to let their own brains dehydrate for the cause
of justice now.

In a world where it is possible to make body-positive
feminist cooks our icons of political empowerment but
vegans the ultimate solipsists or virtue-signalling fools, it can
be hard to get a grip on when and how the act of eating
should be thought of as politically relevant. And yet it is easy
as soon as we think of how our relationships with food do
or don't make political action more possible, urgent or desir-
able. Dolores Huerta, like Weil, has been known to claim
an interest in suffering, in ways that might on the surface
seem excessive, fetishistic. Throughout much of her career
as a leader in the United Farm Workers' struggle, she and
Chávez swore themselves to a life of poverty, hunger . . .
vegetarianism, even. Huerta has joked about her 'exotic
wardrobe', collected by donations alone; she recalls watching
her daughter get confirmed in a pair of torn tennis shoes
full of holes. But Huerta's drive to experience something of
a farmworker's struggle did have a political purpose: it was

intended as a constant reminder of how much was at stake in her efforts as a labour activist.

Huerta's bid for suffering was always connected with her readiness to work towards the cause of social justice. When she called on people not to eat lettuce, eat grapes, drink wine, it was in part to generate economic pressure, and also in part to instil in non-labourers a small sense of the unnecessary sacrifice demanded of farmworkers. 'If we ask people to come and join us for a couple of hours on a Friday and Saturday,' she insisted, 'that's nothing compared to what a farmworker has to do to put food on their table.' Her invitation to share in a modicum of suffering was meant as a form of radicalisation. It was suffering, but always in the service of work that aimed towards painless abundance.

There are things that are very hard to understand, but sometimes it helps to try. Attempting to understand why I could no longer eat, despite all those years of having done it, revealed to me a sickness, not so much in myself, but in our misappropriation of food. For by treating food as a mere means of self-creation, ignoring its power to create new worlds, we turn food into a means of distancing ourselves from social life, rather than entering into it. When an anorexic attempts to cleanse herself of the world by refusing its food, is she not in some way mirroring the social ideal of the 'conscious' eating enthusiast? The so-called 'foodie', who insists that his elevated tastes, his ethically calculated choices, distinguish him from the mass-produced, ultra-processed mob? If either figure, in their shared moral purity, is engaged in a refusal, it is one that takes us nowhere. Or at least no further from the issues that constitute food injustice itself: worker and animal exploitation on a global-industrial scale; the dispossession of farmers; the malnourishment of the poor; the colonial weaponisation of hunger.

This is a shame, since causes worth protesting do not care about moral purity. BDS, for example, does not hesitate to call upon people from nations with bloody hands to take a stand against a nation with bloodier ones. In the imperial core – the place where I learnt to eat – it is much too late for the pretence to moral innocence. The point of BDS is to exert the most pressure on policies that deny Palestinians life; it is a form of solidarity we can easily show and promote; one that Palestinian society has asked for.

To think of any kind of eating as 'easy' has not come easily to me. I suspect there are many more people than have ever been called *disordered* for whom the same would be true. It has taken several years, three hits of mushrooms, two psychedelic guides, a gong bath, a book idea, the subsequent research, the example of political heroes and a political movement worth joining to build in me the inspiration to live that was also inspiration to eat; the inspiration to eat that was also inspiration to live. Surely, you would think, there was a more straightforward way.

The political Left has long been sceptical of any project of 'healing', distinguishing this kind of self-soothing from meaningful political work. Healing oneself, supposedly, diverts us from the fundamental project of transforming the world that makes us ill. Would that it were so simple to commit to the cause; to summon all that faith in its value. As Proctor observes in *Burnout*, if we are to strengthen ourselves for struggle, we must nourish our minds and we must learn to properly mourn. To treat psychic distress and the effort to make it better, she writes, as separate from political work, 'neglects the gravity of the mental strains that arise from living in the world and trying to change it'.

This was precisely the Black Panthers' insight when they set up free health clinics, not to make up for the ills of the world, but to fortify those whose ill bodies belonged to revolution.

At a time when mainstream healthcare was in crisis, as has become its perpetual state, the Panthers joined a loose collection of grassroots groups and organisations in setting up new kinds of decentralised medical services. This radical movement did more than plug a great gap in mainstream health provision – it redefined the very meaning of health, not as bland functionality but a source of mental power. Rather than treating patients themselves as the origin of disease – individual bodies gone haywire – this movement connected the health of every person to their social and political environment. By modelling a new environment – one with collectivised sources of care – they hoped to heal and empower simultaneously.

In 1965, when the first community health centres in the US were established in Massachusetts and Mississippi, the underlying assumption was that you couldn't fix someone's body without also fixing their poverty. The Panthers took this logic further by insisting that poverty, hunger, unemployment, poor education and inadequate housing lay at the root of physical illness. As with their Free Breakfast Programme, which showcased the right to food until the state took it seriously, the free clinics came along with an addition to the Panthers' guiding Ten-Point Programme. To such demands as 'Freedom', 'Full employment', 'Land, Bread, Housing,

Education, Clothing, Justice and Peace' was added the demand 'that the government must provide, free of charge, for the people, health facilities which will not only treat our illnesses, most of which have come about as a result of our oppression, but which will also develop preventive medical programs to guarantee our future survival'.

Food, I have found, can allow us to do more than merely survive. In its pleasures (the use of the erotic), it can raise our expectations of what makes a good life. When food or feeding is violent, it can teach us a healthy disgust for violence more broadly. I still avoid meat, not because it is impure, but to remind me not to tolerate brutality. When I indulge in food, it is not because I feel I have earnt it with my grace, but because it is everybody's right to do so. When I feed others, it is not to bewitch them into becoming fatter than me, but because I want us all, eating, to feel this rightful pleasure; because feeding each other seems like the kind of thing we'd do in the world I would like to believe in.

I do not eat, as it were, for comfort. There is no viable comfort from the awareness of wage stagnation, ambient inflation, insecure housing, insecure jobs, attacks on reproductive rights, neo-fascism, neo-feudalism, neo-colonialism, climate catastrophe, racism and genocide. I eat because contributing to a better world requires that you live, and that you thrive.

I myself, for one, do not always contribute well. There are things that in recent years have drawn me back into myself – disappointments political and personal, stresses financial and existential; the loss, after so much eating, of that little fish I never would feed. Still, I eat because I trust in times when I will be drawn back out again, when I will want to have been kept in running order. I eat because it allows me to continue asking questions of the world; not because I have healed from having to ask them.

I do not eat because I have to, or because I have been taught that it is simply the right thing to do. I do not believe that living itself is any moral obligation, if somebody would rather not do it. I believe, however, in the urgency of making a world that we might all want to live in, something to which many of the people included in this book committed their lives. Some were strengthened by their meals to try and imagine a liveable world; others inspired to try and make living irresistible. All I can say for myself is, when I make it to a protest, I normally bring a sandwich.

Acknowledgements

This book owes all its bold claims to the bolder actions of political radicals past and present. It would not exist at all were it not for the work of comrades in the London Right to Food movement, and in particular Sharon Noonan-Gunning and the Southwark contingent. Worldwide, coalitions of food justice advocates and organisers are 'shoving at the thing from all sides'; it is for readers to explore the causes and organisations that move, and might be moved by, them.

Thank you to agents Angelique Tran Van Sang and Alison Lewis for getting excited when the book was only an email, and to editors Helen Conford and Jenny Xu for doing the same when it was only a proposal. Thanks to all four of you for seeming to stay that way throughout the entire process, keeping me alert, inspired and unafraid. I cannot imagine a more insightful and supportive team to have at the heart of things.

Thanks also to the wider teams at Hutchinson Heinemann and Atria Books. At Hutchinson Heinemann: Laura Brooke, Lindsay Davies, Alice Dewing, Emily Fish, Ania Gordon, Laurie Ip Fung Chun, Rachel Malig, Amy Musgrave, Nicky Nevin, Vanessa Phan, and Hannah White-Steele. At Atria: Ife Anyoku, Molly Berry, Lexy East, Pam Grant, Navorn Johnson, Debbie Norflus, Aleaha Renée, Katie Rizzo, and Claire Sullivan.

Thank you to my friends – lovers of life all. In particular, thank you to Izzie Sunnucks, who for over fifteen years has been asking me the questions I didn't know needed to be asked, and to Tom Stewart and Lucy Brownridge, who have sat through all the most difficult times, while also being responsible for some of the best.

I am grateful to Matt Huxley and Circle Dance for making the confluence of politics, food and revelry a regular and precious feature of my life, as well as many others'.

Thank you to my two cosmic traveller-clinicians, whose care for me exemplified curiosity and respect in a field where the shaming and dehumanisation of patients remains the norm. I am deeply grateful, also, for Penny Georgiou – a spiritual and intellectual guide for life, and to my grandmother, Marjorie Husain, whose love and wisdom – hallucinated and otherwise – I carry with me always.

The will to live is a political matter, but it is also a simple matter of belonging. For mine, I owe my family – Jamil, Erica, Sami and Leila Husain, with whom I will always belong.

I am also thankful to my family out-of-law – Ros, Chris and Dom Huxley – for being a second home.

Thank you, Matt. Friend, boyfriend, comrade, favourite artist, muse. To eat with you is one of the greatest pleasures I have known.

Notes

PROLOGUE

p. 1   *'Tell me what you eat, I will tell you what you are'*: Jean-Anthelme
        Brillat-Savarin, *The Physiology of Taste*, trans. Anne Drayton,
        London: Penguin, 1970 [1825], p. 13.

p. 1   *'hold [his] own in conversation with men of science'*: ibid., p. 21.

p. 2   *'faculty of thought'*: this phrase comes from Brillat-Savarin's
        account of how 'men of science' first analysed food. 'They
        noted its influence even on the faculty of thought, whether the
        mind was affected by the senses, or responded itself without
        the cooperation of its organs . . .': ibid., p. 51.

p. 2   *'clean and solid' ideal . . . 'glitter and ostentation of feudal
        magnificence'*: Max Weber, *The Protestant Ethic and the Spirit of
        Capitalism*, London & Boston: Unwin Hyman, 1930 [1905], p. 171.

p. 2   *'the alibi food gives itself'*: Roland Barthes, 'Towards a Psychosoci-
        ology of Contemporary Food Consumption', originally published
        as 'Vers une psycho-sociologie de l'alimentation moderne', in
        Annales: Économies, Sociétés, Civilisations, September–October 1961,
        pp. 977–988. Reprinted in translation in Carole Counihan, Penny
        Van Esterik and Alice P. Julier (eds), *Food and Culture: A Reader,
        Fourth Edition*, Oxford and New York: Routledge, 2019, p. 18.

p. 3   *Hilde Bruch and . . . Salvador Minuchin*: Bruch was the author, in
        1973, of *Eating Disorders: Obesity, Anorexia Nervosa, and the Person
        Within*, which some still consider a definitive work. The ideas

in it were distilled and thereby popularised in her 1978 book *The Golden Cage: The Enigma of Anorexia Nervosa*. Salvador Minuchin was a pioneer of family therapy, who contributed (with Bernice L. Rosman and Lester Baker) to the writing of *Psychosomatic Families: Anorexia Nervosa in Context*, published in 1978.

p. 4   *Kim Chernin . . . the financially ruinous fate of the wife*: see Chernin's bestseller *The Hungry Self*, published in 1985.

p. 4   *Susie Orbach . . . the subservient female without any needs*: see Orbach's *Hunger Strike: The Anorectic's Struggle as a Metaphor for our Age*, first published in 1986.

p. 6   *'We'd like to believe that such unhinged myopia . . .'*: Alice Gregory, 'Anorexia, The Impossible Subject', *New Yorker*, 11 December 2013.

p. 7   *Dr Agnes Ayton . . . excessive need for control*: as quoted in Sarah Marsh, 'Doctors Warn of "Tsunami" of Pandemic Eating Disorders', *Guardian*, 11 February 2021.

p. 7   *'People who end up with eating disorders tend to be anxious . . .'*: quoted in Lisa Damour, 'Eating Disorders in Teens Have "Exploded" in the Pandemic: Here's What Parents Need to Know', *New York Times*, 28 April 2021.

p. 9   *'moral insanity'*: Henry Maudsley quoted in Lisa Appignanesi, *Mad, Bad and Sad: A History of Women and the Mind Doctors from 1800 to the Present*, London: Virago, 2008, p. 109.

p. 10   *'cognitive-interpersonal treatment'*: Ulrike Schmidt, Tracey D. Wade and Janet Treasure, 'The Maudsley Model of Anorexia Nervosa Treatment for Adults (MANTRA): Development, Key Features and Preliminary Evidence', *Journal of Cognitive Psychotherapy: An International Quarterly*, Vol. 28, No. 1, 2014, p. 50.

p. 10   *'information processing styles'*: ibid., p. 49.

p. 10   *'history taking takes time and reveals little of note'*: ibid., p. 48.

p. 11 *The environment was essentially one of Total Administration*: I refer here to Herbert Marcuse's conceptualisation of corporate capitalism as a system of total administration, in which people are managed by, among other things, bureaucratic ideology and imperatives to perform their optimal function. See Herbert Marcuse, *One-Dimensional Man: Studies in the Ideology of Advanced Industrial Society*, first published in 1964.

p. 12 *'flogging a dead horse'*: 'The Maudsley Model of Anorexia Nervosa Treatment for Adults (MANTRA)', p. 57.

p. 16 *'top-down predictive networks'* . . . *'self-referential processing'*: Abigail Calder et al., 'Psychedelics in the Treatment of Eating Disorders: Rational and Potential Mechanisms', *European Neuropsychopharmacology*, Vol. 75, 2023, p. 4.

p. 18 *'common unhappiness'*: I refer here to Freud's famous suggestion to one of his patients that 'much will be gained if we succeed in transforming your hysterical misery into common unhappiness'. See Sigmund Freud, 'Studies on Hysteria', 1893–95, *The Standard Edition of the Complete Psychological Works of Sigmund Freud*, Vol. 2, London: Hogarth Press and the Institute of Psychoanalysis, 1955, p. 305.

p. 20 *'How do we resist a system we cannot see, a system we are told does not exist?'*: Cynthia Cruz, *Disquieting: Essays on Silence*, Toronto: Book*hug Press, 2019, p. 14.

p. 21 *'insane . . . inhumane'*. 'Anorexia, The Impossible Subject'.

p. 21 *'prefer to categorise their condition as a saintly protest . . .'*: *Mad, Bad and Sad*, p. 430.

p. 21 *'escape from the role of citizen . . .'*: Emmeline Clein, *Dead Weight: Essays on Hunger and Harm*, New York: Knopf, 2024, p. 65.

p. 21 *'touched with understanding'*; *'bodies of imprisoned animals'*; 'Why do I hate everything?'; *'bills and coins and plastic'*: Chris Kraus, *Aliens & Anorexia*, Los Angeles: Semiotext(e), 2000, p. 147.

p. 21   *'intellectual equation between a culture's food and the* entire social order': ibid., p. 141.

p. 21   *'[o]nce all the good girls are dead, who does she want writing?':* Dead Weight, p. 66.

p. 21   *'put mayo on a chunk of bread instead of dying':* ibid., p. 67.

p. 22   *'I want to sit cross-legged and talk about the thoughts that almost killed us . . .':* ibid., p. 7.

p. 23   *'The starving girl, whatever the origin of her symptoms':* quoted in Mad, Bad and Sad, p. 438.

p. 25   *'no natural item of food that signifies anything itself':* 'Toward a Psychosociology of Contemporary Food Consumption', p. 15. Barthes offers as an exception 'such items as salmon, caviar, truffles, and so on, whose preparation is less important than their absolute cost'.

CHAPTER I: YOU DON'T

p. 33   *'trying to make meaningful psychological changes . . .':* unspecified researcher quoted in Todd Tucker, *The Great Starvation Experiment: Ancel Keys and the Men Who Starved for Science*, Minneapolis: University of Minnesota Press, 2008, p. 200.

p. 34   *'slackers':* Congressman Joseph Starnes of Alabama, quoted in ibid., p. 53.

p. 35   *'willingness to subordinate personal interests, activities and welfare . . .':* reported in Ancel Keys et al., *The Biology of Human Starvation, Vol. II*, Minneapolis: University of Minnesota Press, 1950, p. 915.

p. 39   *'Everyone else was pulling down the world'; 'We wanted to build it up'; 'significant work':* quoted in Leah M. Kalm and Richard D. Semba, 'They Starved So That Others Be Better Fed: Remembering Ancel Keys and the Minnesota Experiment', *Journal of Nutrition*, Vol. 6, No. 136, 2005, p. 1348.

p. 40 *'For the rest of my life, people are going to ask what I did during the war . . .'*: quoted in *The Great Starvation Experiment*, p. 168.

p. 40 *'suicide bombers inside the bourgeois nuclear family'*: Lisa Appignanesi, *Mad, Bad and Sad: A History of Women and the Mind Doctors from 1800 to the Present*, London: Virago, 2008, p. 430.

p. 40 *'rebellious and selfless'*: Emmeline Clein, *Dead Weight: Essays on Hunger and Harm*, New York: Knopf, 2024, p. 16.

p. 42 *'I confess that I can hardly bear to contemplate the thought . . .'*: undated letter written some time between Weil's arrival in London in December 1942 and her admission to Middlesex Hospital in April 1943. Evidence suggests it was written around late January 1943. Reproduced in Richard Rees (trans. and ed.), *Seventy Letters: Personal and Intellectual Windows on a Thinker (Simone Weil: Selected Works)*, Eugene, Oregon: Wipf and Stock, 2015, p. 177.

p. 43 *'killed and slain herself by refusing to eat'*: on Weil's death certificate, the physician recorded, 'Cardiac failure due to myocardial degeneration of the heart muscles due to starvation and pulmonary tuberculosis. The deceased did kill and slay herself by refusing to eat while the balance of her mind was disturbed.' Reproduced in Neal Oxenhandler, 'The Bodily Experience of Simone Weil', *L'Esprit Créateur*, Vol. 34, No. 3, 1994, p. 87.

p. 43 *'It's easy to see you've never gone hungry'*: recalled by Simone de Beauvoir in *Memoirs of a Dutiful Daughter*, Harmondsworth: Penguin, 1963 [1958], p. 239.

p. 43 *'I cannot eat the bread of the English without taking part in their war effort'*: letter to Maurice Schumann cited in *Seventy Letters*, p. 177.

p. 44 *'make their own history'*: Weil's critique of Marx paraphrases his doctrine that 'Men make their own history, but in determined conditions'. See Robert Sparling, 'Theory and Praxis: Simone Weil and Marx on the Dignity of Labour', *The Review of Politics*, Vol. 74, No. 1, 2012.

p. 44 *'They need that their life should be a poem'*: Simone Weil, 'The Mysticism of Work', in *Gravity and Grace*, London and New York: Routledge, 2003 [1947], p. 180.

p. 44 *'The transcendent bread is the bread of today'*: from Weil's New York Notebook, 1942, reproduced in Richard Rees (trans. and ed.), *First and Last Notebooks: Supernatural Knowledge (Simone Weil: Selected Works)*, Eugene, Oregon: Wipf and Stock, 2015, p. 102.

p. 44 *'All the desire which nature has placed in the human soul . . .'*: ibid., p. 136.

p. 44 *'Ask that God may transform our flesh into Christ's flesh . . .'*: ibid., p. 265.

p. 45 *'decide with no small amount of pressure from catechism lessons . . .'*: Rudolph M. Bell, *Holy Anorexia*, University of Chicago Press, 1985, p. 115.

p. 45 *'The holy anorexic rebels against the passive, vicarious, dependent Christianity . . .'*: ibid., p. 116.

p. 45 *'to overcome all bodily sensations'*: I am quoting Bell's account here; see ibid., p. 25.

p. 45 *'no longer had need of food'*: Raymond of Capua, *Legenda*, quoted in ibid., p. 25.

p. 45 *'legitimises her defiance and places her in a position of enormous strength'*: ibid., p. 116.

p. 46 *'remarkable'*; *'honourable'*; *'The pure taste of the apples'*: letter to Weil's parents dated 9 June 1943. Reproduced in *Seventy Letters*, p. 189.

p. 46 *'an excess of physical suffering'*: in Weil's London Notebook from 1943, she speaks of how the illusion of pleasure disappears 'at certain moments, brought on by an excess of physical suffering'. She writes: 'One then sees one's existence naked, as a mere fact in which there is no good whatsoever. This is frightful. And that is the truth. (Therefore, may I experience many such lessons and never forget the existence they teach).' *First and Last Notebooks*, p. 358.

p. 46 *'Do please tell me the truth. A little pleasure is necessary in this world, like bread and water . . .'*: letter dated 31 May 1943. Reproduced in *Seventy Letters*, p. 186.

p. 48 They *'rambled over the Sussex downs . . .'*: Rachel Holmes, *Eleanor Marx*, London: Bloomsbury, 2015, p. 117.

p. 49 *'geometric proportions'*: letter to Ludwig Kugelmann, 4 August 1874. Reproduced in *Letters to Dr Kugelmann*, *Lenin Collected Works*, Vol. 12, Moscow: Foreign Languages Publishing House, 1962, pp. 104–12.

p. 50 *'depression overcome, appetite regained, engaged in matters of the world at large'*: *Eleanor Marx*, p. 123.

p. 52 *'a child could scarcely live on it'*; *'untanned skin'*; *'there is a greater criminal than he . . .'*: Eleanor Marx, 'The Irish Dynamiters', *Progress*, May 1884.

CHAPTER 2: YOU RESTRICT

p. 58 *'anti-Semitic Jew'*; *'self-hating black'*: Naomi Wolf, *The Beauty Myth: How Images of Beauty are Used Against Women*, New York: Harper Collins, 2002 [1991], p. 199.

p. 58 *'inert relationship to feminism'*; *'frozen in motion'*: ibid., p. 208.

p. 60 *express themselves 'appropriately'*; *'see the world from other people's perspective'*: Ulrike Schmidt, Tracey D. Wade and Janet Treasure, 'The Maudsley Model of Anorexia Nervosa Treatment for Adults (MANTRA): Development, Key Features and Preliminary Evidence', *Journal of Cognitive Psychotherapy: An International Quarterly*, Vol. 28, No. 1, 2014, p. 50. These are specific objectives of the treatment's Module 7: 'The Emotional and Social Mind'.

p. 60   'battles'; 'calling on a higher authority'; 'If you choose not to eat now . . .':
Janet Treasure, Gráinne Smith and Anna Craine, *Skills-Based Caring
for a Loved One with an Eating Disorder: The New Maudsley Method,
Second Edition*, London and New York: Routledge, 2017, p. 207.

p. 60   'Integrity is doing the right thing when nobody is looking': from
a table of 'Mottos and Metaphors for Different Stages in
Therapy', in 'The Maudsley Model of Anorexia Nervosa Treatment for Adults (MANTRA)', p. 63.

p. 61   'Remember, with anorexia it is as if an "anorexic minx" is sitting on the
chair . . .': *Skills-Based Caring for a Loved One with an Eating Disorder*,
p. 205.

p. 61   'stupid, fat bitch': ibid., p. 206.

p. 61   'the enemy of everything good and decent in the human spirit';
'Hezbollah-like splinter faction': Anthony Bourdain, *Kitchen
Confidential: Adventures in the Culinary Underbelly*, London:
Bloomsbury, 2013, p. 78.

p. 62   'The Dark Side of Veganism': Jessica Brown, 'The Dark Side
of Veganism: How the Diet Can be a Cover for Disordered
Eating', *Independent*, 16 September 2018.

p. 62   'My Vegan Diet Looked Healthful on the Outside: Here's What
Nobody Knew': article by Jamie Kahn, *Huffpost*, 10 February 2022.

p. 62   'I Went Vegan to Hide My Eating Disorder': Rebecca Hills, quoted
on the BBC website, 10 February 2019.

p. 65   *Hitler . . . was perfectly happy to fill up on liver, ham and game*:
see R. H. Schwartz, *Judaism and Vegetarianism*, Herndon, VA:
Lantern Books, 2001, p. 149.

p. 66   'stimulating'; 'those parts of the system which would be better
restrained': J. H. Kellogg, *Ladies' Guide in Health and Disease:
Girlhood, Maidenhood, Wifehood, Motherhood*, Battle Creek,
Michigan: Good Health Publishing Co., 1892, p. 142.

p. 67 *'capricious'*: ibid., p. 176. Kellogg writes that at puberty for women, 'the appetite is often capricious, and frequently new and strange appetites are developed which need to be restrained'.

p. 67 *'A young lady who has ruined her digestion does not want more meat . . .'*: ibid., p. 220.

p. 67 *'nutritive injections'; a 'solution' of pancreas and meat*: see ibid., p. 659.

p. 68 *'Archimedian lever'*: quoted in Adam D. Shprintzen, 'The Vegetarian Crusade: The Rise of An American Reform Movement', 1817–1921, Chapel Hill: University of North Carolina Press, 2013, p. 65.

p. 69 *'gushed and sparkled and danced'*: American Vegetarian Society, 'The Connection Between Diet and Disposition', in *American Vegetarian and Health Journal*, Vol. 1, No. 6, June 1951, p. 114.

p. 69 *'live long and be intellectual'*: American Vegetarian Society, 'Diet and Education', *American Vegetarian and Health Journal*, Vol. 1, No. 5, May 1851, p. 100. The original text reads, 'Parents, if you want your children to live long and be intellectual, live naturally yourselves; put from your tables the "flesh pots of Egypt", and every kind of unnatural food; eat two meals a day; be temperate and abstemious.'

p. 69 *'great mass'; 'degradation'*: J. H. Hanaford, 'Live to Eat vs Eat to Live', ibid., p. 91. Hanaford writes, 'It is lamentable to see how far we are plunging into the depths of degradation and misery, by our excesses; and humiliating to see how low are the aims and aspirations of the great mass, even in an enlightened land and age.'

p. 69 *'crammed with animal abominations'; Such people 'can no more appreciate lofty moral and intellectual teachings . . .'*: 'Exciting Week in New York', *The Liberator*, Vol. 23, No. 37, 16 September 1853, p. 146.

p. 69 *'woman, from an unjust demand of society . . .'; 'ceaseless odor of surloins . . .'; 'the sweet fragrance of myriads of flowers'; 'pure air of rural retreats'*: J. H. Hanaford, 'Women's Sphere', *American Vegetarian and Health Journal*, Vol. 1, No. 6, June 1951, p. 103.

p. 70 *'mangled flesh'; 'vitiated appetites'*: quoted in 'The Vegetarian Crusade', p. 69.

p. 71 *'Experiment'* . . . *and let yourself judge the results*; *'the dogmatism of most "Vegetarians"'*: Eustace Miles, *Failures of Vegetarianism*, London: Swan Sonnenschein & Co., 1902, p. 35.

p. 72 *'live as strictly as you like while you are by yourself . . .'*: Eustace Miles, *The Eustace Miles System of Physical Culture: With Hints As to Diet*, London: Health & Strength Limited, 1907, p. 103.

p. 72 *'impure-blooded'*: *Failures of Vegetarianism*, p. 27.

p. 72 *'unclean'*: *The Eustace Miles System of Physical Culture*, p. 101.

p. 72 *'Many people do best without breakfast . . . A biscuit can be taken at midday'*: *Failures of Vegetarianism*, p. 89.

p. 72 *'You should wish to be healthy, not from a selfish motive only . . .'*: *The Eustace Miles System of Physical Culture*, p. 103.

p. 73 *'conversion'; 'reducing my impact on the living world'; 'We can withdraw our consent from this corruption . . .'*: George Monbiot, 'I Converted to Veganism to Reduce my Impact on the Living World', *Guardian*, 9 August 2016.

p. 74 *'For vegan influencer and bestselling author Ed Winters . . .'*: 'Ed Winters Shares Why He's Compelled to Champion Vegan Activism', V-Land UK, 17 January 2023, www.v-landuk.com/article/ed-winters-shares-why-he-s-compelled-to-champion-vegan-activism

p. 77 *'constitutional rheumatism'; 'I realised, too, that all these years I had caused untold suffering . . .'*: Constance Lytton, *Prisons and Prisoners: Some Personal Experiences*, London: William Heinemann, p. 2.

p. 78 *'spontaneous joy most refreshing'*, ibid., p. 7.

p. 78   *'gaolers . . . great cuff in the face'*; *'How often women are held in contempt . . .'*: ibid., p. 13.

p. 79   *'the spirit behind this movement'*: ibid., p. 15.

p. 79   *'It is a strange fact that the ranks of militant suffragettes . . .'*: quoted in Leah Leneman, 'The Awakened Instinct: Vegetarianism and the Women's Suffrage Movement in Britain', *Women's History Review*, Vol. 6, No. 2, 1997, p. 271.

p. 79   *'for the great majority of vegetarians, the question is not . . .'*; *'either as respected fellow-workers, or simply as companions in the joy of life'*: Élisée Reclus, 'On Vegetarianism', *The Human Review*, January 1901.

p. 80   *'the awakened instinct which feels the call of the sub-human . . .'*: Charlotte Despard, *Theosophy and the Women's Movement*, London: Theosophical Publishing Society, p. 44.

p. 80   *'monster of industrial capitalism'*; *'bridled'*; *'servant of humanity'*; *'fellow worker in the day-to-day glory of creation'*: *Prisons and Prisoners*, p. 4.

p. 80   *'How amazingly they played the game of incessantly advertising the cause . . .'*: ibid., p. 15.

p. 82   *'put ugliness to the test'*: ibid., p. 239.

p. 83   *'much more than necessary'*: ibid., p. 269.

p. 83   *'At first it seemed such an utterly contemptible thing to have done . . .'*: ibid., p. 270.

p. 83   *'Prisoners are made to feel in the presence of nearly every prison official that they are scum of the earth . . .'*: ibid., p. 281.

p. 84   *'difficulties expressing emotion'*; *'blank-faced, reserved and stoical'*; *'enigmatic and bland'*: 'The Maudsley Model of Anorexia Nervosa Treatment for Adults (MANTRA)', p. 58.

p. 84   *'borderline substance'*: A term used to describe nutritional products that have been specially formulated to manage medical conditions. For the relevant discussion of the use of these for vegans, see Royal College of Psychiatrists, British Dietetic Association and BEAT, 'Consensus Statement on Considerations for Treating Vegan Patients with Eating Disorders', March 2019.

p. 87 *'It takes violence to produce moderation'*: Ethan H. Shagan, *The Rule of Moderation: Violence, Religion and the Politics of Restraint in Early Modern England*, Cambridge University Press, 2011, p. 18.

p. 88 *'establish good food habits and follow them . . .'*; *'I'll be proud, too, of being a strong American'*: General Mills, *General Mills Nutritional Study Kit*, Minneapolis: General Mills, 1941.

p. 88 *'authoritarianism in education and political practice'*: Committee on Food Habits, 'Manual for the Study of Food Habits', in Report of the Committee on Food Habits, Washington, DC: National Research Council, 1945, pp. 24–25.

p. 89 *'democratic social engineering'*: see Charlotte Biltekoff, *Eating Right in America: The Cultural Politics of Food and Health*, Durham, NC: Duke University Press, 2013, p. 63.

p. 89 *'allow them to make correct health decisions'*: The WHO defines educational interventions as having the aim of 'improving [individuals'] knowledge and skills to allow them to make correct health decisions', cited in Sergio Ladrón-Arana et al., 'Efficacy of Educational Interventions in Adolescent Population with Feeding and Eating Disorders: A Systematic Review', *Eating and Weight Disorders*, Vol. 28, No. 1, 2023, p. 69.

p. 90 *'the therapist constantly has to maintain the momentum . . .'*: 'The Maudsley Model of Anorexia Nervosa Treatment for Adults (MANTRA)', p. 50.

p. 90 *'reduces the use of healthcare'*; *'minimising the general burden of the condition'*: 'Efficacy of Educational Interventions in Adolescent Population with Feeding and Eating Disorders', p. 69.

CHAPTER 3: YOU GORGE

p. 93 *'roasted not boiled'*; *'spit of the cross'*: Letter 266 in Piero Misciattelli (ed.), *Letters of Catherine of Siena*, Vol. 4, Siena: Giunti & Bentivoglio, 1913–1922, p. 175; and Letter 52 in ibid, Vol. 1, pp. 242–43. Quoted in English in Caroline Walker Bynum, *Holy Feast and Holy Fast: The Religious Significance of Food to Medieval Women*, Oakland: University of California Press, 1987, p. 177.

p. 94 *'such delight that your very body, which for my sake you have denied . . .'*; *'Never in my life have I tasted food or drink sweeter or more exquisite'*: Raymond of Capua, *Life of Catherine of Siena*, Part 2, Chapter 4, Para. 162, quoted in *Holy Feast and Holy Fast*, p. 171.

p. 94 *'there was no other means for man to be satisfied'*: Catherine of Siena to a laywoman, Letter 87 in *Letters of Catherine of Siena*, quoted in *Holy Feast and Holy Fast*, p. 176.

p. 94 *'I want better and more beautiful food'*: *Life of Juliana of Cornillon*, Book 1, Chapter 2, quoted in *Holy Feast and Holy Fast*, p. 116.

p. 97 *'We might be hogging the Earth's resources and tormenting the global working class . . .'*; *Everyone, in other words, 'wants to be rich . . .'*: Barbara Ehrenreich, 'Lowfat Capitalism', *Wise Traditions in Food, Farming and the Healing Arts*, Winter 2002.

p. 102 *'After any evening of carousing, this dish of eggs cooked . . .'*: 'Nigella Lawson's Eggs in Purgatory', *Observer*, 24 January 2017. First published in Nigella Lawson, *Nigellissima*, London: Vintage, 2012.

p. 103 *'I have nothing to declare but my greed'*: Nigella Lawson, *How to Eat: The Pleasures and Principles of Good Food*, London: Vintage, 1998, p. 4.

p. 103 *'You are entitled to eat'*: 'Nigella Lawson on Food, Feminism, and Men in the Kitchen', conversation with Charlotte Druckman, *The Cut*, 18 October 2018.

p. 104 'When I eat chocolate, I linger over every square . . .'; '[A]t no time do I want to carry on . . .'; Nigella Lawson, *Cook, Eat, Repeat: Ingredients, Recipes and Stories*, London: Vintage, p. 33.

p. 104 'extravagant . . . [but] never wasteful': ibid., p. 35.

p. 104 'Gourmandism combines the elegance of Athens, the luxury of Rome, and the delicacy of France'; '[It] unites careful planning with skilled performance, gustatory zeal with discrimination . . .': Jean-Anthelme Brillat-Savarin, *The Physiology of Taste*, trans. Anne Drayton, London: Penguin, 1970 [1825], p. 55.

p. 104 'deserve nothing but praise and encouragement': ibid., p. 133.

p. 104 'by no means unbecoming in women; it suits the delicacy of their organs . . .': ibid., p. 136.

p. 104 'there is no more charming sight than a pretty gourmand in action': ibid., p. 137.

p. 105 'kamikaze'; 'I honour the King, but I can't be him'; 'restore the fragmenting self': Nigella Lawson, *Nigella Bites*, London: Vintage, 2001, p. 140.

p. 106 'mind-numbing obliteration': *Cook, Eat, Repeat*, p. 33.

p. 107 'obscene overindulgence'; 'You want to feel full and grateful but you don't want to be a bloated wreck': Nigella Lawson on *The News Agents* podcast, 'Christmas Special with Nigella Lawson and Ruth Rogers', 22 December 2022.

p. 107 'impassioned, reasoned and habitual preference for everything which gratifies the organ of taste'; 'enemy of excess': *The Physiology of Taste*, p. 55.

p. 107 'It is well known that savages eat to excess . . .': ibid., p. 120.

p. 110 'small vacation from the will': Lauren Berlant, 'Slow Death (Sovereignty, Obesity, Lateral Agency)', *Critical Inquiry*, Vol. 33, No. 4, 2007, p. 779. Berlant describes how 'the body and a life are not only projects but also episodic sites of intermission from personality, of inhabiting agency differently in small vacations from the will itself, which is so often spent from the pressures of coordinating one's pacing with the pace of the working day, including times of preparation and recovery from it'.

p. 110 *'meaningful or meaningless feeling of well-being'*; *'Paradoxically, there is less of a future when one eats without an orientation towards it'*: ibid., p. 779.

p. 112 *'[The] internal requirement towards excellence which we learn from the erotic . . .'*: Audre Lorde, 'Uses of the Erotic: The Erotic as Power', in *Sister Outsider: Essays and Speeches*, Berkeley, California: Crossing Press, 2012 [1984], p. 41.

p. 113 *'The sharing of joy, whether physical, emotional, psychic or intellectual . . .'*: ibid., p. 42.

p. 118 *'always full of food and dancing and reefer and laughter and high-jinks'*; *'tiny little jars of red caviar with bright green bibs around them'*; *'Mostly, women sat around in little groups and talking quietly . . .'*: Audre Lorde, *Zami: A New Spelling of My Name*, London: Penguin, 2018 [1982], p. 256.

p. 118 *'alive and pulsing with loud music, good food and beautiful Black women . . .'*: ibid., p. 287.

p. 119 *'an internal sense of satisfaction to which, once we have experienced it, we know we can aspire . . .'*: 'Uses of the Erotic', p. 41.

p. 120 *'men with full stomachs who live in comfortable houses . . .'*: Audre Lorde, 'Learning from the 60s', talk delivered at Malcolm X Weekend, Harvard University, February 1982, in *Sister Outsider*, p. 140.

p. 120 *'[h]ow important it is not to allow our leaders to define ourselves to ourselves . . .'*: ibid., p. 141.

p. 124 *'proximity'*; *'We wanted to be a space for strong, independent women . . .'*: Transcript of 'Doris Alexander Interviewed by Kelly Anderson', Voices of Oral History Project, Sophia Smith

Collection, Smith College, Northampton, MA, 20 March 2004 and 22 October 2005, Southold, NY, p. 27; p. 35.

p. 125 *'smothered in butter'*; *'creamy and rich'*; *'strictly for garlic lovers'*; *'chancy'*; *'cloyingly sweet'*; *'too salty'*; *'bedecked with more crisp bacon than at most places'*; *'does not skimp on feta cheese'*; *'mighty with mushrooms'*: Linda Wolfe, 'Among Friends: Three New Village Places are Flourishing in the Restaurant-as-Salon Tradition', *New York Magazine*, 14 May 1973, p. 100.

p. 125 *'Obviously to survive we all had to compromise to some degree'*: quoted in Alex Ketchum, *Ingredients for Revolution: A History of American Feminist Restaurants, Cafes and Coffee Houses*, Montreal: Concordia University Press, 2022, p. 84.

CHAPTER 4: YOU FEED

p. 131 *'you told us had to come or we / die'*: All quotations from Diane di Prima's *Revolutionary Letters* are from the Silver Press collection, published in London, 2021.

p. 133 *'romantic'*: di Prima writes, 'A teacher, a path, belonged to some long-gone romantic age, to far-away places like India. It had nothing to do with me in New York City in 1962. Or so I had felt.' *Recollections of My Life as a Woman*, New York: Viking, 2001, p. 319.

p. 134 *'festive'*: ibid., p. 312.

p. 135 *'Absolutely avoid the most Yin vegetables . . . potatoes, tomatoes and eggplant'*: George Ohsawa, *Zen Macrobiotics: The Art of Rejuvenation and Longevity*, Los Angeles: The Ohsawa Foundation, 1965, p. 28.

p. 136 *'The food felt good inside of me, I could digest it, I knew that much'*: *Recollections of My Life as a Woman*, p. 419.

p. 136 *'I began to look for the structures on which I could hang my own experience . . .'*: ibid., p. 421.

p. 140 'going to get sick': ibid., p. 156.

p. 141 'the quiet unquestioned living and dying . . . material pleasures, easy securities . . .': ibid., p. 79.

p. 141 'wondrous girl-cousins': ibid., p. 295.

p. 141 'extended family'; 'No telling how many of us would pile in together, especially in the winter . . .': di Prima writes of this time: 'I had come into my own in a way. Had found a large extended family, many loves.' Ibid., p. 126.

p. 142 'either you want a kid or you don't': Hélène Cixous, 'The Laugh of the Medusa', Signs, Vol. 1, No. 4, 1976, p. 890.

p. 142 'fullness, as if there were more of me than I needed or could use in myself': Recollections of My Life as a Woman, p. 157.

p. 142 'No child is hungry who is not your grandchild . . . no child is orphaned who is not your son': Diane di Prima, 'Haiti, Chile, Tibet', in The Poetry Deal, San Francisco, City Lights Foundation, 2014, p. 76.

p. 142 'joyful'; 'opening'; 'unconquerable': di Prima writes of childbirth as 'being opened from the inside out . . . Now I felt the joy, the power, of being OPEN. Something unconquerable and deep about it. Place from which I live. Twice-torn.' Recollections of My Life as a Woman, p. 190.

p. 142 'gave their love where they wished': ibid., p. 265.

p. 143 'revolutionist gangs'; 'without having to hassle for food'; 'hip food network'; 'beg, borrow, steal and form liaisons': The Diggers, 'The Post-Competitive, Comparative Game of a Free City', The Digger Papers, August 1968, p. 15.

p. 143 'free because it's yours': a slogan used repeatedly by the Diggers. See, for example, 'Selections from the Free City News', The Digger Papers, August 1968, p. 20.

p. 143 *'TODAY IS THE FIRST DAY OF THE REST OF YOUR LIFE';*
'Free food . . .': ibid.

p. 146 *'Take a cop to dinner this week and feed his power to judge . . .':* The
Diggers, 'Take a Cop to Dinner Cop a Dinner to Take a Cop
Dinner Cop a Take', *The Digger Papers*, August 1968, p. 14.

p. 147 *'bullied and bribed into taking "one more bite" of a detested food'; 'a*
woman restricted from acting on anything else . . .': Adrienne Rich,
Of Woman Born: Motherhood as Experience and Institution, New
York: W. W. Norton & Company, 1976, p. 6.

p. 147 *'both a numinous figure and the incarnation of evil'; 'hoard of ambiv-*
alences': ibid., p. 102.

p. 147 *Silvia Federici:* see *Caliban and the Witch*, New York: Autonome-
dia, 2004.

p. 148 *Diane Purkiss:* see *The Witch in History: Early Modern and*
Twentieth-Century Representations, London: Routledge, 1996.

p. 149 *'whimsically married a bitch'; 'won't eat clams, or duck, or*
asparagus . . .'; 'hates children and wants none. Had a successful
miscarriage . . .'; 'this is how it would be when a woman comes to
dinner in another woman's house': Diane di Prima, 'What I Ate
Where', from *Dinners and Nightmares*, New York: Corinth
Books, 1974, p. 13.

p. 150 *'endless witch-hunts':* Diane di Prima, 'Inaugural Address', in *The*
Poetry Deal, p. 3.

p. 150 *'mature woman, almost three years older than her husband . . .':* trial
transcript, p. 2453, quoted in Anne Sebba, *Ethel Rosenberg: An*
American Tragedy, London: Orion, p. 168.

p. 150 *'worse than murder':* trial transcript, p. 2449, quoted in ibid.,
p. 167.

p. 150 *'love for their cause dominated [the Rosenberg's] lives'; 'even greater*
than their love for their children': trial transcript, p. 2453, quoted
in ibid, p. 168.

NOTES

p. 151 *'ten minutes of nursing on each breast; burp 'em and put them back down . . .'*: as recalled by di Prima in *Recollections of My Life as a Woman*, p. 23.

p. 152 *'I wept for the soft and vulnerable flesh things of the world . . .'*: *Recollections of My Life as a Woman*, p. 23.

p. 155 *'when one's whole being says "yes" to a painting, a piece of music . . .'*: ibid., p. 422–3.

p. 155 *'How unlike our concept of the elements . . . separate and distinguishable, static and unchanging'*: Diane di Prima, 'Paracelsus: An Appreciation', in Grossinger, Richard (ed.), *The Alchemical Tradition in the Late Twentieth Century*, Berkeley, CA: North Atlantic Books, 1983, p. 26.

p. 155 *'the one unique mother of all mortal things'*: ibid., p. 29.

p. 155 *'You will grow / a thousand times in the bellies of your sisters'*: 'Revolutionary Letter #2'.

p. 155 *'[W]hat right have you got to breathe out just because you breathed in and there are already too many babies in ny'*: 'What I Ate Where', in *Dinners and Nightmares*, p. 21.

p. 156 *'to live without struggle, or to have a different relationship with struggle'*: *Recollections of My Life as a Woman*, p. 267.

p. 158 *'tone of passionate urgency'; 'the taste of possibility'*: ibid., p. 78.

p. 159 *'one wrote one's dreams, but didn't try to make them happen'; 'grace of possibility'*: 'Inaugural Address', in *The Poetry Deal*, p. 2.

p. 161 *'The way to be a cook is to cook'*: quoted in Warren Belasco, *Appetite for Change: How the Counterculture Took on the Food Industry*, New York: Cornell University Press, 2007, p. 45.

p. 161 *'a living weapon in yr hand'*: 'Rant' ('Revolutionary Letter #75').

p. 161 *'good hot stew . . . ripe tomatoes . . . fresh fruit'*: see Charles Perry, *The Haight-Ashbury: A History*, New York: Random House, 1984, p. 94.

NOTES

p. 162 *'festive communal banquets'; 'elegantly served'; 'where no one is hungry . . . where everyone shares their music, their food, their vision with everyone else'*: 'Inaugural Address', in *The Poetry Deal*, p. 13.

p. 162 *'mothering against motherhood'*: see, for example, Sophie Lewis, 'Mothering Against Motherhood: Doula Work, Xeno-hospitality and the Idea of the Momrade', *Feminist Theory*, Vol. 24, No. 1, pp. 68–85.

p. 162 *'What happened folks?'*: 'Inaugural Address', in *The Poetry Deal*, p. 15.

p. 162 *'Proposition not opposition'; 'proposals for a new society, based on a new consciousness . . .'*; The Diggers, 'A Speech, Dialectics of Liberation', *The Digger Papers*, August 1968, p. 4.

p. 163 *'old ladies'; 'brothers'*: The Diggers, 'The Diggers' Free City, 1968', *The Digger Papers*, August 1968, p. 15.

p. 163 *'puttering over all that brown rice while the guys go off to create the new world'*: Robin Morgan quoted in *Appetite for Change*, p. 81.

p. 163 *'Ruined'*: Caliban and the Witch, p. 80.

p. 164 *'teachers and rulers'; 'Servants and Slaves'; 'England is not a Free People till the Poor that have no Land have a free allowance to dig and labour the Commons, and so live as Comfortably as the Landlords that live in their Inclosures'*: William Everard et al., *The True Levellers' Standard Advanced*, 1649.

p. 165 *'first free the space, goods and services. Let the theories of economics follow social facts'*: The Diggers, 'Trip Without a Ticket', *The Digger Papers*, August 1968, p. 3.

p. 167 *'beers and tears'*: the reference comes from the entry in 'What I Ate Where' on West 16th Street – 'where susan went to live with her lover: beer, mostly, and tears, hardly ever both at once'. *Dinners and Nightmares*, p. 25.

p. 168 *'I won't promise / you'll never go hungry . . .'*: Diane di Prima, 'Song for Baby-O, Unborn', quoted in 'Inaugural Address', in *The Poetry Deal*, p. 2.

CHAPTER 5: YOU ASK

p. 169 *the proportion of UK households without enough food rose from 9 per cent to over 15 per cent*: The Food Foundation, 'A Crisis Within a Crisis: The Impact of Covid-19 on Household Food Security', March 2020 to January 2021, p. 6.

p. 169 *15 per cent more people than before . . . struggling to feed ourselves*: Stephan Zipfel, Ulrike Schmidt and Katrin E. Giel, 'The Hidden Burden of Eating Disorders During the Covid-19 Pandemic', *Lancet*, Vol. 9, No. 1, 2022, p. 9.

p. 171 *'left melancholic'; 'what is in general possible'*: Walter Benjamin, 'Left-Wing Melancholy', *Screen*, Vol. 15, No. 2, 1974, p. 30.

p. 175 *to 'dump the leftover food on the party'*: Elaine Brown, *A Taste of Power: A Black Woman's Story*, New York: Doubleday, 1992, p. 157.

p. 175 *The Panthers used this kind of ingenuity . . . to feed 15–30,000 hungry children each day*: estimate given in Analena Hope Hassberg, 'Nurturing the Revolution: The Black Panther Party and the Early Seeds of the Food Justice Movement', in Hanna Gartha and Ashanté M. Reese (eds), *Black Food Matters: Racial Justice in the Wake of Food Justice*, University of Minnesota Press, 2020, p. 88.

p. 175 *'the most magnificent food giveaways . . . major community events'*: *A Taste of Power*, p. 276.

p. 175 *'to show the community and the government "This is what a just society should do." In a just society . . .'*: Judy Juanita in conversation with Lisa Hix, 'Black Panther Women: The Unsung Activists Who Fed and Fought for Their Community', *Collectors*

Weekly, 12 February 2016, reproduced in Judy Juanita, *Virgin Soul*, Oakland, CA: EquiDistance Press, 2017 [2013], p. 358.

p. 176 *'Survival pending revolution'*: a slogan used frequently by the Black Panther Party.

p. 176 *'The more the party sharpened the contradictions between haves and have-nots . . .'*: *A Taste of Power*, p. 156.

p. 176 *'Your body belongs to the revolution so you have to take care of it'*: Norma Armour Mtume cited in Alondra Nelson, *Body and Soul: The Black Panther Party and the Fight Against Medical Discrimination*, Minneapolis: University of Minnesota Press, 2011, p. 94.

p. 178 *'You have a responsibility to farmworkers because farmworkers feed you'*; *'Fast! Don't eat lettuce. Don't eat grapes. Don't drink wine . . .'*; *'a farmworker has to walk thousands of miles in his lifetime to feed you'*: transcript of a speech given by Dolores Huerta at Stanford University, May 1974. Reproduced in Stacey K. Sowards, *¡Sí, Ella Puede!: The Rhetorical Legacy of Dolores Huerta and the United Farm Workers*, Austin: University of Texas Press, 2019, p. 115.

p. 179 *'implies new social relations free of oppression and inequality . . .'*: La Via Campesina, entry on Food Sovereignty under 'About La Via Campesina', viacampesina.org.

p. 182 *'catastrophic'*: according to the Integrated Food Security Phase Classification (IPC).

p. 182 *a quarter of pregnant women in Gaza were eating only one type of food and more than half eating only two*: 'Israel is Starving Gaza', B'Tselem, 8 January 2024.

p. 183 *According to the Red Lines Policy, Palestinians warranted 37 per cent fewer fruits and vegetables than Israelis, 19 per cent less meat and 43 per cent less dairy*: Visualizing Palestine, 'On the Red Lines Policy', visualizingpalestine.org.

p. 184 *'No electricity, no food, no fuel'*: Rushdi Abualouf and Oliver Slow, 'Gaza "Soon Without Fuel, Medicine and Food" – Israel Authorities', BBC website, 9 October 2023.

p. 184 *'Unfortunately there was a tragic case of our forces unintentionally hitting innocent people'*: Kathryn Armstrong, Emily Atkinson and Rushdi Abualouf, 'World Central Kitchen Halts Operations in Gaza After Strike Kills Staff', BBC website, 2 April 2024.

p. 184 *'tragedy'*; *'done enough'*: 'Statement from President Joe Biden on the Deaths of World Central Kitchen Workers in Gaza', *White House Statements and Releases*, 2 April 2024.

p. 185 *'sent by God'*; *'people on the border who we cannot even send subsistence food items to'*: quoted in Nihal El Aasar, 'Left-Wing Melancholia: The Arab Political Subject', *Parapraxis*, November 2024.

p. 185 *'collective paralysis'*; *'counterrevolution, regional warfare, tens of thousands of Arabs killed . . .'*: ibid.

p. 186 *'If we are to die ourselves, and first to lose in death those who are dearest to us . . .'*: Sigmund Freud, 'Beyond the Pleasure Principle', 1920, *The Standard Edition of the Complete Psychological Works of Sigmund Freud, Vol. 18*, London: Hogarth Press and the Institute of Psychoanalysis, 1955, p. 45.

p. 186 *'the only unifying force in this highly fractured place'*; *'eventually bring Jerusalemites together, if nothing else will'*; *'four thousand years of intense political and religious wrangling'*; *'positive side'*; *'some fantastic food and culinary creativity'*; *'There is something about the heated, highly animated spirit . . .'*: Yotam Ottolenghi and Sami Tamimi, *Jerusalem*, London: Ebury, p. 12.

p. 187 *'suggest that the conflicts they chronicle are perpetual ways of life, crises without origins and without end . . .'*: N. A. Mansour, 'The Rise and Folly of the Refugee Cookbook', *The Counter*, 21 October 2021.

p. 188 *'expose people to a side of Israel [which has] nothing to do with politics'*: quoted in Wilfred Chan, 'A Protest Against a Top Israel-Born Chef Was Called Antisemitic. Staff Tell a Different Story', *Guardian*, 8 December 2023.

p. 188 *'aspire to live in a more just world, with no ranking and suffering, no hierarchy of human worth . . .'*: Omar Barghouti, 'Why I Believe the BDS Movement Has Never Been More Important Than Now', *Guardian*, 16 October 2023.

p. 191 *'meaningful business impact'*: Reuters, 'McDonald's CEO Says Several Markets in Middle East Impacted by Conflict', 4 January 2014.

p. 192 *'exotic wardrobe'*: quoted in *¡Sí, Ella Puede!*, p. 108.

p. 193 *'If we ask people to come and join us for a couple of hours on a Friday and Saturday, that's nothing . . .'*: transcript of a speech given by Dolores Huerta at Stanford University, May 1974.

p. 195 *'neglects the gravity of the mental strains that arise from living in the world and trying to change it'*: Hannah Proctor, *Burnout: The Emotional Experience of Political Defeat*, London and New York: Verso, 2024, p. 40.